YOU
MAKE THE
CALL

CHOICES THAT MAKE OR BREAK US

Dr. Ralph Carter

AMBASSADOR INTERNATIONAL
GREENVILLE, SOUTH CAROLINA & BELFAST, NORTHERN IRELAND
www.ambassador-international.com

You Make The Call

Choices That Make or Break Us
© 2015 by Dr. Ralph Carter

ISBN: 978-1-62020-513-6
eISBN: 978-1-62020-419-1

Typesetting by Hannah Nichols
eBook Conversion by Anna Riebe Raats

AMBASSADOR INTERNATIONAL
Emerald House
427 Wade Hampton Blvd.
Greenville, SC 29609, USA
www.ambassador-international.com

AMBASSADOR BOOKS
The Mount
2 Woodstock Link
Belfast, BT6 8DD, Northern Ireland, UK
www.ambassadormedia.co.uk

The colophon is a trademark of Ambassador

ACKNOWLEDGEMENTS

Thanks to a wonderful church. Brushy Creek Baptist Church has been my home for twenty-three years. I love the people dearly, and they have been more gracious and loving to me than I ever thought possible. I am truly a blessed man. Thank you for allowing me to preach what I felt led to preach, completely unhindered.

Many thanks as well to all of those people who serve in our office. Thank you for letting me take your time to bounce ideas off of you and for all the ideas you give me in return. I am certain you will see some of your thoughts if you read this book. Please don't come after me for plagiarism.

Without the assistance of my administrative assistant, Patti Alexander, this book would have never seen the light of day. Thank you for your input, help in editing and positive appraisals.

My wife, Regina, our children—Angela, Matthew, Carla—and our granddaughter, Scout, are the centerpiece of my life. I hope you know how much I love you and value your insights, encouragements, and advice. Regina thank you for not letting a dream die and for having the courage to get in my face when I was about to throw in the towel. My kids are all techno savvy—I suspect they get it from me. I am a killer at Pong! Their advice as to how to use social media to make people aware of this book has been quite helpful. Scout, thank you for being as beautiful on the inside as I think you are on the outside. My life has been way more fun since you arrived eight and a half years ago. Nothing lifts my spirit like spending an afternoon with you.

Finally, many thanks to my dad. This book has much to do with character and integrity, and my dad is the epitome of these qualities. All my life I've known I could take what he said to the bank!

This book is dedicated to the memory of my mother who passed away in June of 2014. She was such an encourager to me and all my family. You've seen people who are good at just about everything they do—well, that's not me. I have never been blessed with that much talent. But my mother never would admit that. She kept telling me, right up until her death that "I could," when I was convinced of the very opposite. The last trip of any length that my mother made was to endure a drive to Columbia, SC, to hear me preach, just months before her death. She wasn't up to the trip, and I begged her not to come, but she came anyway. She wanted to support her son, like she did every one of her children and grandchildren. It hurt me to see her there in that condition, but it encouraged me beyond words that she and my dad would come. Dad, thank you for the kind of round-the-clock care you provided for her in those last few months of her life. I will forever be in your debt.

Though I told my mother often that I loved her, it never satisfied my longing for her to know how much she meant to me. Though I've made my living speaking for over forty years, I never discovered words that would adequately express what I felt in my heart for her. Moma, I do love you and miss you more than anyone will ever know. Thank you for teaching me that I have a choice. I don't have to do anything by default. I am free to choose what I will do with my life.

CONTENTS

PROLOGUE

CHRISTMAS DAY, 2013, WAS THE worst day of my life. I stood outside my mother's room at Anderson Memorial Hospital, in South Carolina, and listened as a doctor told my family that my mother had Multiple Myeloma, a form of cancer. She was in the final stage of the disease. The next six months would be harder still as I watched this sweet woman, who I have always loved more than life itself, slip away from me.

As I watched her life come to an end, I became more reflective than perhaps I ever had been. I began to think back over the forty years I have been a pastor. In that time frame I have counseled literally thousands of people. I've seen the best of the best and the worst of the worst. I've marveled at how some people can rise up out of dire circumstances to accomplish the unbelievable and watched in equal astonishment as some, despite all the advantages they were afforded, couldn't seem to ever get it right.

I looked more closely at my mother's life than I ever had before. She was never afforded all of the opportunities that my parents gave me. Her father was away for several years in World War II, and she grew up in the leanest of times, serving as equal parts mother to her three siblings as she did a sister. My mother married when she was a sophomore in high school and gave birth to me while my dad was in Korea fighting for our nation. Though she never attended college, she raised three children, during which time her husband was deployed three times for a year-long tour of duty.

I assure you, she was one tough, independent gal.

My Moma (the way I spelled her name ever since I was old enough to write) was the most encouraging, kindest, strongest, and most contented person that I have ever known. Her husband, children, and all of her grandchildren virtually worshipped her. If anyone had ever said a disparaging word about her in our presence, they wouldn't have gotten out alive!

As I watched her lay in a bed at her home, and later at hospice, I wondered so many times, how can she be so kind to everyone who comes and goes, while I, at times, could be so hateful? How is it that she has always been so content and I have always been so discontent? How is it that I can lose my cool and say what I'm thinking in spite of who it may hurt and she always manages to know when to refrain from speaking another word? And that's when it dawned upon me. It's all about choices. My mother lived well because she made good choices, one after another. She wasn't kind by accident. It wasn't just a temperamental trait with which she was born. She chose to be kind, just like she chose to be content, to be an encourager, or to be strong. The course of our lives is not determined nearly as much by where we are born, or to whom, or about the advantages we are afforded, but rather about the everyday choices we make.

And that is why I am writing this book—I've spent my life trying to point people in a direction that would enable them to live life well—to make fewer mistakes—to live life, as the writer of Proverbs puts it, "skillfully." The key to living such a life is to make good choices. It's not rocket science, nor is it dumb luck. It is all about choosing well.

CHAPTER ONE

"YOU DECIDE, I DON'T CARE"

DO YOU EVER GET WEARY of making choices? Bet you do. Open a restaurant and call it, "I Don't Care, Wherever You Want to Go," and you will make a mint. Whenever I ask my wife, that's her favorite place in town. Ever thought about why we say that so often? It's because we are so weary of making choices we could scream. The demand to make decisions seems to never end!

As if things weren't bad enough, decision making is getting harder with the passing of every new day. It's a lot more difficult today than when I was a boy growing up in the fifties and sixties, because there are so many more options today than there were then.

When it came to food, the choice was not where or what, but how much were you going to eat? You were eating at Mom's and you were eating whatever she fixed. Believe it or not, there were no golden arches in the south in the fifties. McDonalds, which began on the west coast, didn't open its 100th restaurant until 1960. Within a decade that would radically change, and in the decade following it would explode. The choices at lunch today are endless. Mexican, Italian, Chinese, Japanese, Indian, Cuban, French, German—you name it, and we have it. A quick glance at the number of restaurants in even a small city reveals that Americans love to eat out. Who would have ever thought in the fifties and sixties that there would be more restaurants than clothing stores, banks, or service stations?

And what about cars? As a teenager I could recognize virtually every car made. In fact, most of my

> *Life is all about the choices we make.*

buddies could tell you the make, model, and year of practically any car out there. Today, no one can do that, including the salespeople. Where once the differences between makes and models were clear cut, today they are marginal at best. Unless you notice the emblem of the company, good luck identifying most of them.

When you watched TV you picked from ABC, NBC, or CBS. No need for a remote; it was *Gunsmoke, Bonanza,* or *Gilligan's Island.* Today you can have 250 channels and still not find anything you care to watch. News is reported twenty-four hours a day as well, thanks to Ted Turner and CNN. As a result, they no longer just report the news—they create it.

You can watch cooking, pawning, restoration, picking, or somebody trying to sell you a juicer anytime you want. Want to see sharks in business suits or from inside steel cages? We've got you covered. How about an hour of watching two adults running around in the jungle getting their fannies eaten off by mosquitoes and spiders? No joke, we got it.

Get the point? Decision making has become more difficult in part because our choices have increased exponentially. Thankfully, some of the decisions we make don't make a lot of difference. But some—many in fact—matter a great deal.

That's why I am writing this book. We make so many decisions they have come to seem unimportant. Lots of times, we make them unaware that we have even decided anything. We make so many choices that we figure they really don't matter much—but they can, and often do.

In fact, here is a summary statement about life that I believe you might find helpful:

LIFE IS A SERIES OF CHOICES.
GOOD CHOICES RESULT IN A GOOD LIFE.

Don't let the simplicity of the statement throw you off. Stop and consider it for a moment. Life is all about the choices we make. Make good ones and you do yourself a huge favor. Make crummy ones and, well, you've got problems. Here's another summary statement, written from a negative perspective but equally true.

BAD CHOICES RESULT IN A LIFE OF MORE
THAN YOUR FAIR SHARE OF BAD DAYS.

Life typically won't be blissful if we occasionally make a good, even great, decision. But please understand that one really bad decision can come pretty close to ruining much of your life. So making good decisions is of utmost importance if you want to live a rewarding, exciting, enjoyable life. And, as important as making good decisions is, avoiding bad decisions is just, if not more important, than making good ones.

QUESTIONS TO TALK ABOUT

1. Do you ever tire of making choices?

2. Which is harder for you to decide: where to have lunch, what to eat when you get there, or what to wear in the morning?

3. If you could eliminate one decision you have to make in the next thirty days, what would it be?

4. Why do you think making decisions is so hard at times?

5. In your opinion, what is the most important factor in making good decisions?

CHAPTER TWO

YOU HAVE A CHOICE!

WHEN WE ARE INFANTS, OTHERS choose for us. They decide what we wear, when we sleep, what we eat, where we go, what we see, and how we are entertained.

As we age, we are afforded the opportunity to make more and more of the choices that impact our lives. Within just a couple of years, with the help of our parents, we begin to make some of the decisions just mentioned. Typically, the better we handle the choices we are afforded, the more freedom we are given in making future decisions. By the time we are eighteen, most of us are making the vast majority of our choices. If, by the time you are out of college, you are not making all your decisions, you have a problem. You may seek the advice of parents, friends, teachers, and pastors, but if you are not the one pulling the trigger on whatever decision is being made, then you need to declare your independence! (Just a word of warning, you can't declare your independence if you are not living independently—translation: "paying the bills.")

So whether you are just now in a position to make all your choices, or you have been at it awhile, here are a few more of those summary statements:

EVERY CHOICE MATTERS.
SOME MATTER MORE THAN OTHERS, FOR SURE.
BUT, EVERY CHOICE MATTERS.

Most people know that, but very few live as though their choices are important. Most of us are pretty careless in making decisions. Why are we flippant about the choices we make? Because we make so many! After a while we forget we even have choices. But we do!

We have a choice about everything—little choices, big choices, choices of consequence, and choices with hardly any consequences. We get to decide to go or stay; to rise and shine or to sleep in and vegetate; to study or to party; and to be polite, or to act like a jerk. It's all up to you. You are in the driver's seat. You will determine the kind of person you will be and the kind of life you will have. The choice is completely yours. And rest assured, the choices just keep on coming.

As a result, most of us get a little haphazard in our choices. At times you will become weary of having to make them and attempt to relinquish control to another. You will flip a coin, ignore or postpone your decision, or respond by saying, "I don't care; you decide." "Whatever you want is fine with me. Suit yourself." "It doesn't matter; I don't give a rip." But ultimately, even your decision to relinquish control, is a choice you have made.

Sadly, there are moments when we become desensitized to the fact that we even have options. We dupe ourselves or allow ourselves to be duped into believing that the only choice we have is the one being forced upon us. But that isn't true! You can choose the road less traveled. For instance, you can choose to do what is best for you—what is most rewarding for you. You don't have to make the obvious choice that we are conditioned to make. You don't have to watch any of the 250 channels. You can turn the TV off. You actually can!

You can sit in silence. For real. You can read a book, build a shelf for your garage, take a walk, or sit on a neighbor's porch and talk. This will blow your mind, but you can

> *You don't have to make the obvious choice that we are conditioned to make.*

even save the $150 a month by getting rid of cable. They aren't the IRS. You don't have to pay them.

You don't have to live in a particular neighborhood to be happy. The divorce rate from one neighborhood to another doesn't vary much. People in the nicest parts of town have troubles too. They eat and drink too much and overmedicate themselves just like folks in the adjoining zip code.

This book is about choices. It is about recognizing exactly what your choices are and making the most of them. I won't attempt to make any of your choices for you. (Honestly, I won't. It's not that I don't care, I just have enough trouble making decisions for myself. Besides, I suspect you are getting enough help with that as it is.) Peer pressure, societal expectations, parental pressure, advertising, the PC police, and our own self-imposed expectations make it difficult for you to even believe you have much of a choice, but you do. So whether you make it or forfeit it to the wishes of another—the choice is yours. I want to help you recognize you have options! You get to decide. The choice is yours. In a nutshell, man, I'm trying to give you your life back. For goodness sake, take it.

QUESTIONS TO TALK ABOUT

1. What is the first real choice you remember your parents allowing you to make?

2. Do you remember the first moral choice you ever made? Can you tell the group about it?

3. Do you ever forfeit your privilege of making decisions?

4. Do you ever allow someone to pressure you into making a choice you really didn't want to make?

5. Can you think of a decision you know you need to make but you haven't gotten around to making it yet? Do you know why you are putting it off?

CHAPTER THREE

GO GET THE LIFE YOU WANT

A PERSON'S LIFE IS DETERMINED, in large measure, by four factors—one's choices, the choices that others make that impact one's life, the circumstances in which one finds himself, and God.

Listen to people explain why their lives turned out the way they did, and if it hasn't gone well, more often than not, they either blame circumstances or the choices others made which impacted their lives. But that isn't true in most instances. If you were to go back and look at every decision they made, I am convinced you would come away persuaded that they were primarily responsible for the course of their lives.

Do circumstances play a role in determining the outcome of my life? No doubt they do. While I determine many of the circumstances in life by the choices I make, there are lots of circumstances over which I have no control. For instance, I can't control where, when, or how I am born, much less to whom. I don't get to choose my family. I can educate myself, but I have no voice in how intelligent I am. I can't control my family's behavior or values. My race, ethnicity, nationality, and living conditions (at least as long as I live with parents or guardians) are all up for grabs. God and parents determine all that.

Likewise, I can't control what others do. Some people will treat me well; others won't. Some are fair and equitable; others are selfish and intolerant. Some people are encouraging; others are mean. Some can be trusted, while others betray our trust.

Then there's God. He unquestionably determines a great deal about the course my life takes. God hasn't pressed the start button and then run off to the wings where He curiously watches to see how things turn out. He hasn't left it entirely to us. He intervenes in our lives. He purposefully had Pharaoh say "no" to Moses' requests to leave Egypt until He was ready for Pharaoh to say "go." What about the fact that Moses was the baby fished out of the Nile and raised in Pharaoh's palace? Coincidence? Really? God orchestrates aspects of our lives. Check the scriptures, and you will find that His hand was on a host of biblical characters before they were ever born. Is there any reason to think His hand has not been on us as well?

> *The outcome of my life is critically dependent on the choices I make.*

He numbers our days, orders our steps, and yet He still allows us to make choices that impact the direction of our lives. At times, He even saves us from our own willful stupidity. Aren't you glad about that?

And lastly, we make choices. Choices about what we want, what we do, how we think, the attitude we have, how we respond to our circumstances, and other's treatment of us. The outcome of my life is critically dependent on the choices I make. Daily we make hundreds of choices, and almost all of them impact our lives—some with little consequence but others dramatically.

Take a look at Samson. Who would have ever imagined he would end up as described in Judges 16:21?

> *The Philistines seized him and gouged out his eyes. They brought him down to Gaza and bound him with bronze shackles, and he was forced to grind grain in the prison.*

Imagine if we could transport Samson in time back to the present. "Samson, how did you get in this shape? What happened? Who is to blame?"

I'd bet the farm that his response would be something like this: "It was that Philistine prostitute, man. She deceived me. She betrayed me."

"Really? So you were doomed? The outcome couldn't have been different?"

Nonsense! Samson could have made a different choice. This didn't "happen" to him. He made a series of bad choices that led to his demise. He chased women all his life and refused to heed his parents' warning not to get mixed up with girls from the enemies' camp. He even ignored the clear evidence that Delilah was bad news, that she would betray him in a heartbeat. In fact, four times she asks him the secret to his strength, and although he lies three times, every time she puts his response to the test. She even demonstrates the unmitigated gall of complaining that he doesn't trust her, in the midst of her betraying his trust.

> *Samson could have made a different choice.*

So no, Samson, I must respectfully disagree. You acted like a dope. You have no one to blame but yourself. You made some incredibly bad choices!

What about Pilate? Pilate was an educated man, the governor of Judea. He was experienced in making decisions. Listen to this exchange between him and a crowd that gathered outside his palace one morning:

> Pilate asking them, "Then what do you want me to do with the One you call the King of the Jews? Again they shouted, "Crucify Him!" Then Pilate said to them, "Why?" What has He done wrong?" But they shouted, "Crucify Him!' all the more. Then willing to gratify the crowd, Pilate released Barabbas to

them. And after having Jesus flogged, he handed Him over to
be crucified. (Mark 15:12-15)

Matthew 27:24 indicates that Pilate felt troubled by his decision.
When Pilate saw that he was getting nowhere, but that a
riot was starting instead, he took some water, washed his
hands in front of the crowd, and said, "I am innocent of
this man's blood. See to it yourselves!"

But try as hard as he might to shift the blame from himself to
the crowd of Jewish antagonists, the choice still belonged to Pilate. It
was his choice then, and it will be his throughout eternity. Was there
intense pressure on Pilate to favor the will of the mob? Of course there
was. But the choice still belonged to Pilate. He tried to get Herod, a
visiting governor from another region, to decide, but Herod wouldn't
bite. In the end, it came down to Pilate's call. He had to make a choice
between freeing a man who he found to be innocent or satisfying the
crowd. He took the easy path. He caved. He had been charged with
making sure justice prevailed and he failed.

**GOOD CHOICES ARE NOT EASILY MADE. BUT THE
CONSEQUENCES OF MAKING BAD DECISIONS
ARE FELT, LONG AFTER THE DISCOMFORT OF
MAKING GOOD DECISIONS HAS PASSED.**

Consider David's decision to seduce Bathsheba. It led to murder,
dishonor and embarrassment, exposure, public humiliation, and the
death of his son. And what about Adam and Eve's decision to succumb
to Satan's temptation? They suffered expulsion from the garden, a
life of heartache and turmoil, hard labor, guilt, and the fall of their
children for a thousand generations to come.

A few months ago I watched as my mother lay in a bed suffering
from cancer that would finally take her life. As tears streamed down

my face, I thought about the heartache caused by Adam and Eve's decision to disobey God. All of us have suffered from their bad choice to obey Satan rather than God. And there is no reason for you or me to think that our children will not suffer from our bad choices as well.

Thankfully, we also have the capacity to make good choices. Joseph, who was sold into slavery by his own brothers, in spite of all his hardships, makes a godly choice in Genesis 39:12. When Potiphar's wife attempts to seduce him, Joseph turns and runs as hard as he could—leaving her rejected and clutching his coat. He made a right choice. Did it pay off for him in the short run? No, life immediately became more difficult. Joseph's righteousness was rewarded by being wrongly accused and cast into prison. The payoff, in the moment was that his relationship with God and integrity remained intact. Good choices are often not easily made.

Let's look at one final character. Joshua, as a younger man, learned the value of making good choices. When he was sent in by Moses to spy out the land that God was giving His people, only he and Caleb returned with a faithful report.

> *Good choices are often not easily made.*

While all the spies agreed the land was a resourceful land, everyone except Joshua and Caleb contended that it was too much for them to expect to be victorious against such a formidable opponent. Joshua and Caleb pled for them to trust God for the victory but to no avail. As a result, for forty years God's people aimlessly wandered in the wilderness until all those who were adults had died. That is, except Caleb and Joshua. Their courageous choice paid off!

It isn't surprising then, when Moses' death comes, God has readied Joshua to take the reins of leadership. Nor does it come as a surprise, that Joshua, as his own death nears, challenges his people to decide who they will obey in life. Joshua knew that you can't make people choose to do anything, let alone follow God. Faith is personal, it must be one's own personal choice. Many parents fall prey to this critical mistake. We can't discipline or force our children to embrace our faith. We can only decide for ourselves who we will serve, how we will live our lives and hopefully inspire our children to follow suit. Here are Joshua's final words to his people.

> But if it doesn't please you to worship Yahweh, choose for yourselves today the one you will worship: the gods your fathers worshiped beyond the Euphrates River or the gods of the Amorites in whose land you are living. As for me and my family, we will worship Yahweh." (Joshua 24:15)

How about you? Have you made a choice as to whom you will serve?

QUESTIONS TO TALK ABOUT

1.   How have circumstances, completely out of your control, determined either by God or parents, impacted your life?

2.   Can you think of a time when you made a bad decision but blamed someone else for the consequences because of the role they played in the outcome?

3.   Without telling this to anyone else, can you determine the worst three choices you ever made? Why do you think you made them?

4.   What were two of the best choices you ever made?

THE BIG CHOICES

Earlier I said, "Every choice matters. Some matter more than others." Well, that's right. Some choices aren't going to follow us around for more than a few hours at most (choosing to put onions on my hot dog). But some (choosing who I marry) are going to impact everything about my life. So common sense would dictate that I should really consider some choices very, very carefully, right? But oddly enough, it appears to me that some people hardly consider some of the weightier decisions we make in life.

For instance, ever heard of people getting married after knowing each other for only a few weeks? Doesn't mean it won't work, but it sure isn't smart. Or how about when a couple is on, no wait, they are off again. Yeah, they are off, no, wait, they are on again. No wait, they are married. Or what about when a couple goes through a painful divorce, and two weeks later they have found their soul mate. For crying out loud, get a puppy!

In the next six chapters, I want to tell you about six choices you can't afford to make without very careful, thoughtful deliberation.

CHAPTER FOUR

CHOOSING YOUR FRIENDS

REMEMBER THE FIRST INVITATION YOU received from someone on Facebook asking if they could "friend" you? Keep in mind, I was born in 1951. It was weird. It took me back to the sixth grade when some girl would pass me a note in a discreet fashion from another girl who was her best friend, saying, "If you like me, check yes, and if you don't, check no." Dog gone it! You're in a bind. If you check no, she's gonna cry. If you check yes, the guys are going to give you a hard time.

I don't know about you but I "accidentally" hit delete until my son, who's more up to date with social media, told me all about Facebook. From then on, I just intentionally ignored them. I've got 3,300 members in my congregation; I've got all the friends I need!

For any of that number that are reading this, relax, I'm just kidding. But, to be honest about it, I'm not a Facebook guy. I hardly ever take pictures and never take them of myself. And frankly, I get annoyed with people who do like taking pictures of me. Additionally, I am not much of a stalker. I see and hear enough bad stuff as it is. So when I'm not paid to listen in on people's private lives, I don't.

But there is one thing about Facebook I like—the part where you are able to "un-friend" someone. How cool is that? With the touch of a key—like the swoosh sound you used to get from AOL when you were notified that "you've got mail"—they are gone. Lost in cyberspace.

Don't get me wrong, everybody needs friends. Good ones are such a gift from God. But frankly, some people are never going to live better, happier, more productive lives, until they lose some of the friends they have.

The Book of Psalms begins with these words:

How happy is the man who does not follow the advice of the wicked or take the path of sinners or join a group of mockers! (Ps. 1:1)

In the book of Proverbs we are admonished numerous times not to get too chummy with hot heads, lazy people, connivers, or the sexually promiscuous.

Good friends are a treasure. The scripture tells us that there are some friends who will stick with us closer than a brother. David and Jonathan had a friendship that has seldom been rivaled. Jonathan placed his friendship with David ahead of both loyalty to his insanely jealous father and any personal ambition he might have had regarding one day being king.

Even Jesus needed and appreciated his friends. He dined whenever His schedule would permit Him with His three friends from Bethany. In His darkest moment He entrusted His dear friend, John, with the responsibility of looking after His mother following His death.

But friends aren't always a blessing. Just ask Job. His three pals nearly sent him off the deep end. They managed to compound the misery of a man already suffering exponentially.

While you need friends, exercise care in choosing them. Friends play a major role in determining the course of your life.

Stay away from a foolish man; you will gain no knowledge from his speech. (Prov. 14:7)

The whole point of Psalm 1, Psalm 15, and a host of other similar passages is that we need to be careful about the company we keep. Friends influence our lives. We pick up their habits—good or bad.

Our friends reflect our comfort zone. Choose virtually anybody, take a look at their friends, and you will quickly realize that the one you have chosen is a cross section of the people they hang out with. Why? We run with folks with whom we are most comfortable. There are no doubt exceptions, but for the most part you can take that to the bank. When there are exceptions, they are usually purposeful. Jesus loved to hang out with sinners. It wasn't that He was comfortable with their sins, but rather that He wanted to impact their lives and appreciated their transparency. In fact, my guess is that He loved it. He saw so much phony baloney religion that, even in their sin, their "realness" and transparency was refreshing.

So should we have friends that aren't the best of role models? That's a good but tricky question.

For openers, we ought to be friendly with everybody. People aren't my enemy just because they don't live the way I choose to live. Sometimes believers have a hard time recognizing that. If I can help anyone then I need to respond as a friend would. Jesus did that innumerable times.

But Jesus never began imitating the behavior of those to whom He ministered. He genuinely loved them and befriended them but He didn't take His cues from them. They never influenced His behavior.

Ideally, we ought to do the same. But I've got to recognize the fact, that I am not Jesus. I am more easily influenced than He was. Satan tried to get Him to take the easy way out after fasting for forty days and nights in the wilderness. Satan did it in a very subtle way as well. But he was no match for Jesus. Something tells me, based on past experience, I wouldn't have fared as well. How about you?

Years ago my dad told me something that I foolishly disputed at the time, but, man, was he right. He warned me about a friend I was hanging out with and said, "Son, I know you have good intentions, but I want to warn you—bad influences good far more often than good influences evil." Unfortunately, I didn't learn that until I became a casualty.

All of us are influenced by the character, choices, and habits of our friends, intentionally or unintentionally. Friends who are honest, kind, spiritually minded, generous, and uphold strong moral values influence us to do the same.

Iron sharpens iron, and one man sharpens another. (Prov. 27:17)

By the same token, people who are dishonest, carnal, worldly, mean spirited, gossips, or hot tempered have a negative impact on their friends as well. Just think about it.

You've heard it said that frogs are cold blooded creatures. Put them in a pot and gradually turn up the heat and they will stay there

> *". . . bad influences good far more often than good influences evil."*

until they roast. Find someone who has never gone to anything other than G rated movies and introduce them to a PG-13 movie. He or she will be blown away by the profanity they hear. But let them attend the theatre for six months and they build an immunity to it. Move them on to R rated movies and the same thing occurs.

Instead of being entertained tonight by the tube, spend an evening watching television as an analyst simply observing all that is said and done. You will be amazed at how much of an appetite for crude, sexually implicit, vulgar language and behavior you have developed over the past few years. Most of our mothers would have thrown the TV out the window when we were children if the things that are being shown today were shown twenty years ago. But those influencing us know that. So Hollywood typically doesn't take quantum leaps, they are content to just get a bit more edgy each year.

So we are influenced by what we allow into our world, and no one influences us more than our friends. That's why they call it "peer pressure."

We pick up not only on their characters but on their habits, both good and bad. Put me daily with people who attend church, pray, read their bibles regularly, love their spouses, enjoy spending time with their children, and I will be more inclined to do the same. But put me on a daily basis with people who drink excessively, do drugs, steal, flirt, cheat on their spouses, or behave lazily, and the chances are that I will develop some of the same habits and my own values will be marginalized.

Friends have the ability to persuade us to do things we wouldn't have ever done on our own. They have influenced me to try new foods, purchase products I had never considered, make investments I would never have made, be stronger in my faith, share the gospel, and take moral stands. But friends can also influence you for evil. A significant number of inmates are in prison because of the influence of a friend. Are they responsible for their actions? You bet—legally and morally. But lots of people have made criminally bad decisions they would never have made had they not been influenced by a friend. They were just along for the ride until things got out of hand and they are left to pay the price for their friend's stupidity.

I've had occasion to go back and consider the four or five worst things I've ever done. (I'm not sure I'd recommend that for you, it's a painful experience.) But in doing so I discovered something pretty astonishing; at least seventy-five percent of those things would have never happened if I had not been influenced by someone else. Don't get me wrong. I made every bad choice I ever made. I am the only one to blame. But unquestionably, I would have chosen a different path had it not been for the influence of "friends." Be careful who you let into your life.

Ahab was one of the most wicked kings to serve Israel, but only God knows how much Jezebel influenced his life (1 Kings 21). Solomon was influenced by his wives to the point that he did unspeakable things.

> *My son, if sinners entice you, don't be persuaded. If they say*
> *–"Come with us!" don't travel that road with them. (Prov. 1:10-11a, 15a)*

Friends can make all the difference in the world, though, when we are going through difficult times.

> *A friend loves at all times, and a brother is born for a*
> *difficult time. (Prov. 17:17)*

After my mother was diagnosed with Multiple Myeloma, for six months we watched her slip away. It was devastating to our entire family. Had it not been for friends, I don't know what we would have done. I am afraid to think of how our family would have handled it had our friends not been there.

I am a very independent person and want to do for myself whenever possible. But in times like those we encountered, I was surprised to find how much we need and depend on our friends. Without ever asking how they might help, they find a way to lighten the load. That's why it is so important that you choose your friends wisely.

May I make a few suggestions in choosing your friends?

Choose individuals who demonstrate character and integrity. Would I trust this person with the life of my little brother, sister, or child?

Choose people whose spiritual values are very similar to yours. Denominational lines and verbal professions don't count for much. But take careful aim on how people flesh out their faith.

Choose friends who give as much as they take. Heed my secretary's advice. "Don't make anyone a priority who makes you an option."

Choose peers who would never want you to violate your conscience or do anything out of your comfort zone. Find friends who are low maintenance, to whom you may say no without explanation.

Choose to hang out with people with whom you may be yourself. Don't spend your life pretending to be someone you aren't for the sake of their approval.

Choose confidants who love you enough to tell you the truth, even if it means jeopardizing the friendship. Friends don't sit by and watch friends ruin their lives out of fear of offending them.

Finally, choose those who will keep loving you, when others have abandoned you.

A man with many friends may be harmed, but there is a friend who stays closer than a brother. (Prov. 18:24)

A few years ago a good friend of mine got in serious trouble with the law. In fact, he is in prison, for a crime he admits he committed. It was in all the papers and every major network called my home and wanted to conduct interviews. Pastors of other churches called and offered their condolences to me. Both in and out of the church people wanted to know, what are you going to do? I was always perplexed by their question.

I did what friends always do, I was a friend. I was at his side in court. I comforted him and his family the best I knew how. I listened and, occasionally when asked, offered counsel. Most importantly, our church poured out love to this man and his family in a way that was nothing short of miraculous.

. . . all of us are the recipients of grace . . .

Why did we respond that way instead of distancing ourselves from him? Because all of us are the recipients of grace and recognize other people's need for it as well. We don't have to condone anything, in order to love somebody.

QUESTIONS TO TALK ABOUT

1. Who was your best friend as a child? Have you remained friends?

2. How do you think that friendship impacted your life or decisions as a kid?

3. What are the traits you look for in a friend?

4. What are the traits that you flee from in a friend?

5. Without stating a name, can you think of a friend you might do well to lose?

CHAPTER FIVE

CHOOSING A PARTNER FOR LIFE

HAVE YOU EVER CONSIDERED THE fact that the first marriage on record was an arranged marriage? Have you ever heard anybody say, "God made her with me in mind?" Well, I don't know if that's true in your case, but it was in Adam's. God caused Adam to fall into a deep sleep and from his side took a rib that He changed into a wife, named Eve. He gave Eve to Adam to be a helper, a partner, and a companion. The only thing about creation that displeased God was that Adam was initially alone. So God provided Adam with a wife.

> *It is far better to be single and looking for Mr. or Mrs. Right than to be married and looking to leave Mr. or Mrs. Wrong.*

It was an idea that caught hold. Since that time, most men and women have sought out partners in marriage. Some have chosen to stay single for a reason, others for a season, and still others because they never met the person they deemed suitable. Marriage, however, is a choice. You don't have to be married to be happy, successful, or fulfilled. It is far better to be single and looking for Mr. or Mrs. Right, than to be married and looking to leave Mr. or Mrs. Wrong.

Some people choose their own mates and others allow their families to choose for them. Most Americans typically scoff at the latter idea as being archaic, but the divorce rates of other cultures compared to our own make one wonder which method is best. I am not proposing that we go back to an ancient tradition, but we should at least see if there is something we can learn from cultures older than our own.

Arranged marriages are brought about by parents. Who loves us more and knows us better than our parents? Parents are older and, thereby, typically wiser (not necessarily smarter) and more cautious than their children. They recognize when their children are treated well versus treated poorly. Believe me, as a counselor, I can assure you that lots of people preparing to be married apparently can't make that distinction. Might a parent be swayed too much by factors that aren't as important as others? They certainly might be. Money, security, stability, and a host of other factors might play into their decision more than it should on occasion. A couple's unseen chemistry might not be as apparent to a parent as a child would want it to be. But the big advantage that I see is that parents, by virtue of having been married, have a pretty good idea of what marriage requires of one another. People getting married for the first time are pretty much clueless. So when they see qualities that are problematic for the future of their child's marriage, you would think they would be extremely cautious.

The heartache of a broken marriage doesn't end with the pounding of a gavel . . .

Let me be clear, I don't want to pick a spouse for my children, nor do I want you to do that. But I do want couples considering marriage to begin being more cautious about making a lifetime commitment. The heartache of a broken marriage doesn't end with the pounding of a gavel in divorce court. The heartache is there for years to come and more often than not, a lifetime. So to ask that we exercise more care in choosing a mate isn't unreasonable at all. Few decisions will ever impact your life more than this one.

SO WHAT SHOULD I LOOK FOR IN A SPOUSE?

I'm a big believer in asking people who've been there and done that, what they think. So a while back I said to the guys and gals in my office, "Hey, you guys have all been married for a long time. If you were marrying again now, in view of what you know about marriage, what would you look for in a spouse?" Let me share with you some of their responses.

"CHOOSE SOMEONE YOU CAN TRUST."

Choose someone you can trust with your darkest secrets, your money, your heart, and your children. Choose someone you believe would never betray your trust and someone you don't have to go around wondering about in regard to their trustworthiness. Choose someone whose words you don't have to interpret.

"CHOOSE SOMEONE YOU LIKE AND WITH WHOM YOU BELIEVE YOU WILL BE LIFELONG FRIENDS."

Loving someone is important but liking them is even more important. Choose someone you miss talking to when they are not around, someone you laugh with, and someone with whom you feel free to share your secrets.

"CHOOSE SOMEONE YOU ADMIRE."

Look for someone you admire spiritually, intellectually, and emotionally. Someone whose work ethic, personality, and ability to get along with others you admire. Don't consider for a second marrying someone who you are ashamed of, or embarrassed by, in any way. It's not fair to you or them.

"CHOOSE SOMEONE WHOSE VALUES SPIRITUALLY AND FINANCIALLY ARE THE SAME AS YOURS."

Don't settle for someone who "can" agree with you, but really doesn't share your values.

"CHOOSE SOMEONE WHO YOU ARE PROUD TO INTRODUCE TO PEOPLE AS YOUR SPOUSE."

Instead of just looking at the exterior package or the financial security that someone offers put a premium on traits like: humility, confidence, dependability, graciousness (ability to forgive others readily), kindness, a willingness to be adventuresome, and good judgment.

The best lists of traits I've ever found in searching for a spouse come from Galatians 5:22-23. These are the qualities that the Spirit of God produces in the life of a believer who is willing to be controlled by God's Spirit.

Love, joy, peace, patience, kindness, goodness, faith, gentleness, self-control. (Gal. 5:22b-23a)

Those are the very traits that Jesus demonstrated, and, anyone who has ever been married will tell you, these are the very traits that will make a marriage work.

By the same token, there are some traits I would keep an eye out for that would make me run like I'd stole something.

If someone threatens you, hits you, or even looks like they'd like to do so but restrains themselves, make it easier for them, run like Forrest Gump. Don't consider for a New York minute anyone who will treat or speak to you unkindly when you are dating. It's going to get worse—I promise! Avoid the guy or gal who is in love with themselves. Being around the insecure is tiring, but hanging out with the boastful will make you nauseated. Nobody likes liars, but amazingly, lots of people marry them—so don't ignore the red flags. Avoid gossips, unless you like a steady appetite of that day in and day out. And put distance between yourself and those who hold grudges against others. Today it's somebody else. After the "I do's," it will be you sooner or later.

> *If they are demonstrating bad behavior now, it is only going to get worse . . .*

The same applies to people who don't like lots of people and are quick to say so. I mean, after all, what's the likelihood you will in time do some of the same things those people are doing? And, by all means, run from stingy people. The time will come when their thriftiness will make you want to kill 'em. It's one thing to manage your money, but it's another to have to get permission to buy a snow cone. And the list goes on. The biggest thing is, don't be stupid. If they are demonstrating bad behavior now, it is only going to get worse once you've married. My goodness, friend, if they are putting their best foot forward right now and they are driving you insane, it's not going to work.

But what if I am engaged and believe I've made a mistake?

Marriage is a choice. *You really can say, "No, I'm not going to marry you. It's off. I don't want to do this."* You may be considering their feelings and don't want to hurt them. Ask yourself, "What is going to hurt more, a cancelled engagement or a divorce." I assure you, there is absolutely no comparison. Don't believe I'm right? Ask some of your divorced friends what it was like.

Remind yourself, until I say "I do," it's NEVER too late to pull the plug on a relationship you know won't work or that you don't want.

Here's one last tip. When I was in seminary a professor told me, "If you ever interpret a passage of scripture and check all the commentaries only to find that no one agrees with your interpretation, don't get excited and feel as though you are the first to see it clearly. Realize, you've made an error." By the same token, if you are about to say "I do" and virtually everybody who loves you is saying "don't," realize you are the one with the flawed judgment. Back away; better yet, run!

QUESTIONS TO TALK ABOUT

1. What would be the five traits you would most look for in a spouse?

2. What are the traits in a potential mate from which you would flee?

3. What would be a few absolute deal breakers, even if you were engaged?

4. What do you believe would be some of the problems you would encounter if you were to ever go through a divorce?

CHAPTER SIX

CHOOSING TO MAKE MY MARRIAGE WORK VERSUS ENDURING IT

NOT LONG AGO I HEARD a comedian say if marriage had to be sold like automobiles, we wouldn't have many people getting married. I have to agree with him. Think about it. Fifty percent of those who have been married couldn't wait to get out of it. I'd bet my lunch money there is at least another twenty-five percent, who, while they haven't opted out, don't think of it as a day at Six Flags either. And to top it all off, the remaining twenty-five percent, who are your cheerleaders for marriage, say things like, "It's rewarding, but, man, you really have to work at it every day." Who buys a car you have to work on every day? Nobody!

So the truth is, marriage is tough. Have you ever thought about why it's so hard?

Here are a few reasons for openers. Two people are put together FOREVER. When I graduated from high school I went to the beach for a week with my best friend. We nearly fist fought before that week was over. I don't care who you are, you have issues! It's hard for anybody to be in the same house with another human day in and day out and not get upset with each other on occasion.

Making things worse still, we often come from different back-grounds, different types of families, different cultures, and increasingly different ethnicities. What's more—in case you haven't noticed—we're selfish. We want things our way. We say it doesn't matter so much of the time, but it is amazing how often it does.

"I don't care where we eat, you choose. I'm not picky; I'll eat any-thing." "OK, what about Mexican?" "No, that stuff gives me indigestion."

Here's another biggie. When you are in your twenties you think, hey man, so long as there's sex, it's going to be alright. But guess what? Marriage is about more than sex. In fact, in the grand scheme of things, it's a pretty small part of everyday life. It's important to be sure, and without a good sex life your days are probably numbered as a couple. But, it's still just a single aspect of marriage.

Another problem with marriage is that after a period of time, we all have a tendency to take each other for granted. We make assump-tions instead of showing appreciation, and feel safe with one another and lose our inhibitions and filters.

And finally, when you are twenty, and someone says, "Marriage is until death do you part," it sounds like heaven, but when you are fifty, "for life" sounds like a prison sentence.

So what are your options? You can divorce, endure it, or make it work. But it is a *choice*. You rarely *have* to divorce.

Admittedly, there are times you do. For the welfare of my children, for my physical safety, or for my financial survival, I might have to divorce. But in most circumstances, I have another option.

Nor, do I want to choose to endure it. Life is too long and too short. Marriage will wear me out spiritually, emotionally, and men-tally if all I do is endure it. I want

> *You can divorce, endure it, or make it work. But it is a* choice.

it to work. I want it to be a blessing to me, my spouse, my children, and my community. It can be. So, despite the problems and there are problems, I want to see it work.

How do I do that? If I came to love my spouse by investing my time, energy, and resources in him or her, I must continue to invest. I must forgive transgressions. I must resolve differences. I must accentuate the positive. I must remind myself of my commitment.

If this is going to work, both spouses need to choose to make it work. I can make our marriage work better just by making some changes myself, but if it is to really work as it should, both of us must work together. So naturally I wonder, what if my spouse refuses to put forth any effort?

Then pray they die young. (Relax. I'm kidding.)

Some people have said, "But Pastor, we've tried everything. We're stuck. We don't know what to do." So let me tell you a few choices that you can make, that I believe will truly make a measurable difference in your marriage.

Begin by examining your personal relationship with God.

Make a conscious choice to maintain a right walk with God. When Joshua could see the end of his life in sight, he called together his people and issued a number of challenges.

> Therefore, fear the Lord and worship Him in sincerity and truth. Get rid of the gods of your fathers . . . choose for yourselves today the one you will worship:. . . . As for me and my family, we will worship Yahweh. (Josh. 24:14a, 15b)

Make up your mind from day one; will we be a Christian home or not? Allow that decision to govern your speech, finances, treatment of one another, child rearing practices, the respect you demonstrate to one another, your demeanor, and your involvement in church. Behaving as a Christian should, solves a lot of problems.

Don't blow off the impact of this choice in favor of less spiritual but more sophisticated solutions. Following this idea will make all the difference in the world in your life and in your marriage. If you are praying regularly, worshipping regularly, reading God's word regularly, and living for Christ daily, you won't just get along with your spouse-- you will get along better with everybody. People who love God as they should, love those around them as well.

Next, choose to live by putting others ahead of yourself. In Philippians, Paul admonishes believers to have the exact attitude in ourselves that Christ had. He put others' interests ahead of His own. In that list of others, no one should be a higher priority than our husbands or wives.

Most arguments occur when we insist on having things our way. In Ephesians 5 Paul tells wives to submit to their husbands just as they did to Christ when they became a believer. Husbands have perhaps an even tougher task. They are to sacrifice themselves for their wives just as Christ did the church when He gave Himself up for her. As I read those passages I don't find much room for making an argument about why I must have my way. Selfishness, like selflessness, is a choice. It is one you can make.

Third, choose to forgive the big stuff and simply ignore the little stuff. Most of us have become entangled in an argument that seems to drag on and on, until we realize, at some point, that we don't even know how it began. That's a sure indicator that an argument isn't very important. It is amazing how we can get all bent out of shape over the silliest of things.

May I make a helpful suggestion? The next time you are tempted to correct, reprimand or criticize your spouse—ask yourself, "Is this something worth ruining a perfectly good day over?" I bet it's not.

There are times when we have to forgive sizeable hurts.

At times, however, our disagreements are not over trite situations. There are times when we have to forgive sizeable hurts. Remember the story of Joseph in Genesis. He was sold into slavery by his brothers. In fact, the idea to sell him only arose as a profitable solution to their real desire to kill him. You may have suffered terribly by the actions of your spouse, or someone else, but most of us cannot fathom the hurt Joseph suffered at the hands of his ruthless brothers. Genesis 45:1-8 tells us that Joseph made a remarkable choice. He chose to forgive his brothers for what they had done. He opted to move on with his life and to salvage what he could from a relationship torn apart by others' jealousy and hatred. The choice is yours. Be angry, lose any opportunity for restoration, or forgive them, as you have been forgiven by God. How do I do that? Forgive them the way you would your children or your grandchildren if they had disappointed you.

Love them for who they are. Your spouse isn't perfect. He or she wasn't perfect when you married them, and you either knew that or chose to ignore it. Here's a news flash—you aren't either! You chose them, so love them for who they are. There was a reason you fell in love with them; search for that reason now.

Choose to love them extravagantly. Want to see a picture of extravagant love? Look at this:

> And a woman in the town who was a sinner found out that Jesus was reclining at the table in the Pharisee's house. She brought an alabaster jar of fragrant oil and stood behind Him at His feet, weeping, and began to wash His feet with her tears.

She wiped His feet with the hair of her head, kissing them and anointing them with the fragrant oil. (Luke 7:37-38)

That's extravagant love, isn't it? But notice something else; Jesus, later in the story after telling a parable, tells us why the woman loved Him so tenderly. It was because she had been shown so much love by Him, when He knew her sins. Extravagant love is usually reciprocated. Stop lamenting how you haven't been loved as you had hoped and begin loving your spouse, the way you want to be loved.

Finally, **choose to seek help before it is too late**.

We hesitate way too long in getting help for our marriages. People typically will tell everybody about their failing marriage except those who could actually help. More often than not, couples are just on the verge of seeing an attorney before they give me a call. Why don't they go to someone for help much sooner than they do? The reasons vary. But the two big P's account for many.

With some, it's pride. They might say, "I don't want anyone to know we are having trouble." When you divorce, Einstein, they will figure it out.

With others, it's about the price. Some couples think, "Those guys charge an arm and a leg for sitting there listening to you tell them about your problems." Have you been to a doctor or dentist lately? Called a plumber to come and get your commode unstopped? Now we're talking big bucks! But if price is keeping you from seeing a professional counselor, call a local pastor before you throw in the towel.

I am a pastoral counselor. Like most other pastoral counselors, I don't charge. But keep one thing in mind. You get what you pay for. My daughter, who is on staff with me and thinks I lack diplomacy and sensitivity, asks me pretty often, "Dad, why would anyone in their right mind, come to you for counseling?" My response is always the same, "Cause I work cheap."

Through the years I've also heard a lot of people reluctant to see a counselor say, "I already know what they are going to say! It will just be a waste of time."

Can I be the first to break this to you? You don't know everything. You aren't right about everything. And what you know about mar-

> *. . . what you know about marriage isn't nearly as important as what you* do *. . .*

riage isn't nearly as important as what you *do* about your marriage. Let someone help you, and don't walk away from marriage without exhausting every possible solution.

The choice is yours. Choose to love your spouse. Choose to make your marriage work, no matter what it takes.

QUESTIONS TO TALK ABOUT

1. Why do you think marriage is so difficult?

2. What is the biggest contributing factor to failed marriages in your opinion?

3. Someone has said that men marry reality and women marry potential. Do you think there is any truth to that? Why or why not?

4. Do you think it is wise to talk to someone other than a professional about your marriage problems? Who would be on the "never" list and who would be on the "maybe" list?

CHAPTER SEVEN

CHOOSING TO AFFAIR-PROOF YOUR MARRIAGE

MORE MARRIAGES FAIL BECAUSE OF infidelity than for any other reason! Period. In my experience as a counselor, nothing else is a close second. People have affairs for a variety of reasons but often times, it isn't for the reason(s) that a lot of people might think.

There are immoral people who never take seriously the commitment they made at the wedding altar. They have no intention of being faithful, and so it's just a matter of time before they find themselves involved in an affair. And, sadly, it doesn't take them very long to do so.

Some having been chasing skirts all their lives (the male version; there is a female version as well). It's what they do—I'm not kidding! It is what they do 24/7/365, and they never stop, so a wedding band isn't going to change that. The minute you realize that's who you are dating, break it off. Don't think you can rehabilitate them; you can't. They are addicted to sex and the chase. Until they get professional help, they are hopeless.

Some, with absolutely no intention of really repenting, convince needy spouses that even though they strayed, it will never happen again. I've even seen some spouses so arrogant, they actually tried, and at times succeeded, in convincing their spouses that they (the offended party) were to blame. Some unfaithful spouses tell their partners, "You got so big when you were pregnant that I didn't find you very appealing." "You got so busy earning a living for our family that you quit telling me how pretty I was." "You quit fixin' up like you used to do, and it's not my fault those women at work look and smell so good all the time."

But believe it or not, about half of the people I see who have had affairs are not who you would expect. They not only seem to be moral people, but they typically are. Most love their children (though they clearly aren't thinking about them), and lots of these people have some feeling of fondness for their spouse (typically they say they don't want to see them hurt). So how and why did they end up having an affair?

I can't tell you the number of times the confessing party has said something like this to me: "I never intended for this to happen. I didn't set out to have an affair. It just happened before I knew it. Pastor, the truth is, my spouse and I have been growing apart for years. We are two different people than when we married. We don't have anything in common, and to be honest, I don't love her/ him anymore. I have feelings for her/him, but I'm not head over heels in love with my wife/ husband like I am this other person. And with this other person it is so easy. We are perfect for each other. We are interested in the same things. I sure wish we had met years ago because I had no intention of hurting my spouse and kids."

Here is what I have discovered over the years: The person confessing is telling a half-truth when he or she says they didn't intend for it to happen.

He is telling the truth when confessing that he and his spouse have been growing apart.

And she is telling the truth when explaining that the relationship started out emotionally and then turned physical. Most moral people don't just jump into bed with someone they don't know. Typically to move to the physical phase of a relationship they have to have some emotional connection, though not always. The less moral conscience they have, the easier an affair becomes.

And finally, it doesn't really matter what people's intentions are; they are going to destroy lives by proceeding with the affair.

What they are unaware of most of the time is this:

It didn't just happen. They set themselves up for it to happen. How? 1) By having a bad relationship at home and not actively doing something to fix it. 2) By flirting with someone of the opposite sex. They would deny that they were

> *It didn't just happen. They set themselves up for it to happen.*

initially flirting, but if they were perfectly honest, they would know that both men and women relate to people of the same sex one way and to people of the opposite sex another way. Let a group of men be huddled up talking and have a woman come up and say virtually anything. Everything about the group dynamic changes. The same is true of a group of women. It doesn't mean that anything sexual is suggested or intended, it's just that the group dynamic changes. Men want to impress women, and women want men to find them attractive. The person in this example, male or female, wanted to be noticed. When he or she was, it felt good. This person was flattered. His or her ego was stroked. In and of itself, that situation may not present a problem. But if that person keeps returning in order to receive that same feeling, "Houston, we have a problem." An unhealthy attraction is formed, that if fed, will invariably lead to an emotional attachment and subsequent affair.

Can this situation be avoided? You bet your life it can. Let me share with you some steps you can take to "affair proof" your marriage.

- Maintain a healthy relationship with your spouse. Work on your marriage daily. If the relationship ceases to be satisfying, immediately seek counseling. In marriage you made a commitment to God, your spouse, your family, and your friends. Don't let the marriage fail because of your lack of effort.

- Wear your wedding band.

- Keep pictures of your spouse and children on your desk if you work in the public marketplace. It serves not only to remind others but also yourself. Lives are at stake here. Don't hurt those you claim to love the most.

- When it comes to choosing best friends, unless it's your spouse, limit your choices to people of the same sex.

- Limit the number of private, personal conversations you have with someone of the opposite sex. The more you talk, the more likely you are to have an affair.

- Don't discuss marriage problems with someone of the opposite sex, unless that person is your marriage counselor.

- Don't engage in conversations about sexual matters with people of the opposite sex. Limit your conversations with people of the opposite sex to those you would be comfortable with your spouse or children overhearing.

- If you feel yourself attracted to someone, be honest with yourself about that and immediately back away. Change your routine; don't wait until things are out of control to take action.

- If you perceive that someone in your circle of friends might be developing feelings for you, back away and make your spouse aware.

- If anyone ever tells you that they have developed feelings for you, let them know that you think it is best that the two of you not associate any further. Do whatever is necessary to put space between yourself and the other person.

QUESTIONS TO TALK ABOUT

1. Do you think it is dangerous for a married person to be the best friend of someone of the opposite sex?

2. Are there any other steps that you believe couples could take to safe guard their marriage?

3. If someone was on the verge of having an affair with someone, where emotional ties had been established, what should he or she do?

4. What do you believe would be the steps a person should take in breaking off an affair?

CHAPTER EIGHT

CHOOSING HOW I SPEND MY MONEY

MONEY IS IMPORTANT! THE MAN or woman who worships it is a fool, but that doesn't diminish its importance. I hear people say all the time that money isn't important to them, but they turn around and prove themselves liars. They hold onto it with clenched fists and hardly give any of it away. They use it to keep score with their friends and family. I hear people who live in mansions talk about how they would be just as happy in a double wide, but they don't ever move to a trailer park. If they would be as happy in a trailer as a mansion, it would seem sensible to move, wouldn't it? I mean they would save a bundle, but then why would they want to save it; they said the money didn't matter anyway. But, I guess they could give it away. Ah, I know why they don't! They are protecting the poor people from becoming as miserable as they are. So I guess that hoarding it is kind of thoughtful of them after all.

Money is kind of weird, isn't it? We want it, but we don't want anybody to know we have it. But we kinda do want them to know or better yet, we want them to suspect we have it. Maybe that's why we run up big credit card bills. We want other people to think we can afford all the stuff we have, when we know we can't. But they don't know that, so when they ask us for some, we can honestly say, "I don't have any." That way, they go away thinking we are just stingy, but not broke.

Yep, money makes us act weird all right!

There must be some kind of unwritten law somewhere that dictates you do stupid things with your money once you start to really get some. I read a book a few years back that was really pretty fascinating. Somebody did a study of what people with a fair amount of money do for fun on the weekends in NYC. They said they went to the theatre; to concerts; to professional ball games; to very pricey, critically

We feel compelled to do those things that are an indication that we've made it, rather than do those things that bring us joy.

acclaimed restaurants; or to expensive out of town weekend retreats. The study then asked these people a second question: what are the things you enjoy doing most in life? Their answers were about as simple as they come. They said they enjoyed going for a walk in the park with their spouse, getting an ice cream cone and sitting on a bench, flying a kite with their kids, tossing a football or Frisbee, or watching a sunrise or sunset. What they do costs boatloads of money; what they like doing costs peanuts. So why would you pay more to enjoy less? Simple. It's about status. We feel compelled to do those things that are an indication that we've made it, rather than do those things that bring us joy.

So why don't we go for that feeling more often? It's simple. We've been duped. We see ad after ad that tells us the fancy sports car is where the joy is. But it isn't—any more than the fancy restaurant, the $100 theatre ticket, or you name it. I am not saying there isn't a time to go to the theatre or five star restaurant. But what I am saying is that we ought to spend our money wisely, in a fashion that genuinely brings us joy, not the appearance of joy.

May I offer some advice on some things you might want to consider as you spend your hard earned money?

Spend your money wisely and thoughtfully. Don't throw it away.

- Use coupons and "groupons" whenever possible. Why not stretch your dollars? If you don't have to spend them, don't. It will allow you to give more away.

- Stop being a big shot. I can't speak for everybody, but excessive spending never impresses me. I always think of little men with big cigars when I see someone throwing money around like it is water.

- Wait for items to go on sale. Sooner or later, virtually everything will. I don't have to be the first to own anything. When items are marked down 75% it means they were initially marked up 300%.

- Don't buy something you don't need or can't afford, simply because it is on sale. You never save when you spend. It is still a deficit, no matter how much of a "steal" it was.

- Use credit sparingly. "The borrower is slave to the lender." I put that in quotations just so you'd know it's not original with me. King Solomon gets credit for that one. Pay off credit card balances at the end of the month; credit card debt kills finances, credit scores, marriages, and dreams. If you can't pay your bill off at the end of the month, forgo buying it with a credit card.

- Learn to appreciate and recall the feeling of being debt free. Remember how the joy of new car ownership is always dampened somewhat with the arrival of a payment book. And even worse, remember what it's like to be out of money before you are out of month? Now those are feelings we can all vividly recall, but we have trouble recalling the feeling that accompanies the lack of indebtedness. Believe me, it's a great feeling to have, especially when compared to its counterpart. Get debt free and fall in love with the feeling that accompanies it.

- Develop the ability to decline invitations you can't afford to accept. Some people who typically spend their money fairly wisely, can suddenly act foolish when someone invites them to do something they know they can't afford to do. Out of fear of embarrassment or a desire to fit in, they accept an invitation they know they can ill afford. Remember, you aren't obligated to give an explanation. Simply say, "Thanks, but I better not." You never owe anyone an explanation about what you can or cannot afford. An apology is never needed for acting responsibly. Individuals, couples, corporations, and nations would all be well advised to recognize when they can and can't afford to do something.

- If you hang out with people who are constantly doing things you can't afford, find new friends. You don't have any right to slow them down, and they don't have any right to put you in debt. If you hang out with people who are financially well above your means, you will either spend money you don't have or will become a freeloader. You don't want to do either of those things. If you have friends who want to include you in activities that you can't afford on your own, it is fine on occasion to be their guest, if they are insistent. Just don't let it become habit forming. People don't like someone living on their dime with a constant presumption of grace. Good friendships can be lost.

Be aware of where your money goes. I can't tell you how many times in counseling I have heard a husband say, "I make great money, but I don't have a clue where it goes. I ask my wife, and she just looks at me with a blank stare. It makes me so mad." Believe it or not, most of the time, there isn't a gambling problem, a drug problem nor is someone squirreling money away for a time when they plan to get out of the picture. Most of the time it's just that they make lots of money and don't know where it goes. They are spending without much thought or deliberation and are spending recklessly, without a plan—in many cases, without a clue!

So they've made a choice with their money; it just wasn't a good one. They chose to spend their money blindly, wildly, and without consideration for what they would really like to do with their hard earned cash.

The solution is simple. Stop! Stop spending your money without knowing where it's going. How do I do that? Invest a buck in a small spiral notepad that fits easily in your shirt pocket, pants pocket, or purse. Don't let it out of your sight for thirty-one days. Take it everywhere you go. Every time you make a purchase, pay a bill, or give a buck or two to your children, write it down. Don't change any of your spending habits to try to "cook the books." Buy the same number of sodas you always have, only this time make a record of it.

You will see where every dime went and you won't have to guess, falsely accuse, or remain in the dark. You will know. Knowing is the only way you can make a conscious, willful decision about what you really want to do with your money. It is your money. You should choose how you spend it, not just surrender it by default!

I can already tell you, you will likely be amazed at how much you spend eating out. Americans eat out today exponentially more than their parents did forty years ago. We convince ourselves that so long as it's not a fancy restaurant, it's not too bad or that it costs about as much to take our lunch to work as to grab a bite here or there. In fact, the amount of money you spend in tips will likely astound you. I am not advocating tipping less, but I am suggesting perhaps you would do well to eat at home more often.

But the bottom line is this—it's your money! So if you want to eat in a restaurant every meal that is perfectly acceptable. Just understand that there may be some other things you would have liked to have done that you won't be able to afford to do. It's all about making a choice.

Avoid catastrophic loss. In times past, many people were "insurance poor." They had more insurance than they needed. Today, if there is a problem regarding insurance, it's that we don't have enough. Make insurance your highest priority in terms of protecting your family financially, to maintain health coverage, even if it is only catastrophic. You can recover with difficulty from the loss of a car, perhaps even a house, but a single health crisis can create financial problems you will never be able to overcome without filing for bankruptcy. Even then, the problems don't just all go away.

When considering a change in jobs, benefits mean more than ever!

Take care of your family. First and foremost, take care of your family (spouse/children/parents/family who can't work, rather than don't work). The Bible has some pretty harsh words for those who don't look after their families. Recognize that you have an obligation to assist aging parents when necessary.

Save regularly. Put aside a portion of your check every payday. Decide on a percentage and don't ever deviate from it, unless it is upward. Discipline yourself to live on a portion of your salary rather than the whole and teach your children to do the same.

Be charitable! The Bible says wonderful things about the generous. But you know what I've found? So does the world. But, nobody says anything good about the stingy. Nobody! Set aside a portion of your salary that you give to charity. Don't be so stingy as to become comfortable spending all you make on you and yours! Never believe those braggarts who talk about being self-made. There isn't any such thing as a self-made man. Even when we aren't keenly aware of who they are, I believe there have always been people in our lives who have helped us out along the way. We need grace and need to demonstrate grace.

Spend your money deliberately and purposefully. As I said in an earlier portion of the book, you don't have to have cable because everybody else does. You can exist without an iPhone, and you can wait until the movie leaves the theater to see it. Sooner or later, they will put that dress or pair of shoes on sale. But the flipside is this, if that's what you genuinely want, then get it. There's nothing sinful about standing outside in sub-freezing weather to be the first to have an iPhone if that's what floats your boat. It's your money, you should decide how you spend every dime of it. Just don't let either an advertiser or a close friend pressure or shame you into spending money you don't have or don't want to spend, on what's been suggested. Choose for yourself what you do with your money.

Stop feeling guilty about spending what you've earned. That is not to say you shouldn't spend your money differently than perhaps the way you are at the moment. It's just to say, it's your money, spend it as you like. Why feel guilty about the trip, meal, car, house, whatever it is you use your money to buy, if you earned it legitimately, have provided for your family's needs, aren't putting your family in future danger financially, are being generous with others, and aren't spending money that God specifically spoke to you about to use for some other purpose? Buy that dress you've had your eye on. Splurge! Take your husband or wife on that cruise! Love your spouse extravagantly! You can't take it with you. If you aren't going to give it away, spend it.

Don't deprive yourself, if you are retired, in order to leave your children money when you're gone. Here's the hard truth about inheritances: some children, even adult children, will waste it, (now that would annoy you, wouldn't it?), some will fight over it, and hardly any of them will ever appreciate it the way you dreamt they would.

Don't get me wrong, you don't have to be in a mad rush to spend it all before you get out of here, but you don't have to do without so they will sing your praises either. I have been a pastor for a long, long time, and I've seen tons of children who have been left considerable amounts and have seen those who weren't left a thing. I can honestly tell you I've never seen the money make a nickels difference in how children in either category felt about their deceased parents. Think about it; would it make any difference in how you feel (felt) about yours? Why would your children be any different?

QUESTIONS TO TALK ABOUT

1.   Have you made a purchase in the last sixty days that you regretted making? Why?

2.   If you had a $100 that you could spare, to what individual or charity would you give it?

3.   If a man has a balance of $3,000 on his credit card and the interest rate is 20%, how long will it take him to pay off his balance if he pays $100 a month?

4.   How much would you estimate you spend in eating out, including tips, on a weekly basis? Would you rather spend your money on traveling to a nice destination annually or eating out several times a week?

5.   Calculate how much money you spend on television and movies annually and ask yourself if there is anything else you would rather do with that amount of money.

6.   If you were adding a couple of do's and don'ts, what would they be?

THE BIGGER CHOICES

In the last six chapters we looked at some really important choices one must make in life. Marriage, career, money—those are issues that most people consider to be the really big choices in life. As big as they are, I believe there are bigger choices still. In fact, these bigger choices, will in large measure determine who we marry, how our marriage plays out, and what kind of success we realize in whatever career choice we make. So far, I have largely written about the external choices we make. In the remainder of the book I want us to look at what I consider more important issues still—the internal choices—what kind of person will I be?

CHAPTER NINE

CHOOSING THE KIND OF PERSON I WILL BE

PEOPLE SOMETIMES MISTAKENLY BELIEVE THAT people of character and integrity are people who were simply born with that disposition. They may think these "perfect people" had to either have been Boy Scouts or never missed a week of Sunday School. But that isn't true. People who demonstrate character and integrity in life, do so because of choices they make. In fact, it isn't one of those "once and done" choices either. They maintain their integrity just as long as they continually decide to do so. That's why we are constantly surprised to hear of someone in the news who has been arrested for something we would never have suspected he might do. "Good" people don't always act as they should, and "bad" people don't always act badly. That's the good part. Every day we live we have the opportunity to make a choice as to the kind of person we will be.

It may sound too simple to believe, but it's true. The **only** thing that separates a person of honor and integrity from a bottom dwelling, scum sucker is a choice—a decision to live honestly.

How do I become a person of honor, integrity, and character?

The Bible gives us some great insight at this point. Listen to what King David writes in Psalm 15:

> Lord, who can dwell in your tent? Who can live on your holy mountain? The one who lives honestly, practices righteousness, and acknowledges the truth in his heart— who does not slander with his tongue, who does not harm his friend or discredit his neighbor, who despises the one rejected by the Lord but honors those who fear the Lord, who keeps his word whatever the cost, who does not lend his money at interest or take a bribe against the innocent - the one who does these things will never be moved. (Ps. 15:1-5)

David raises the question who can live with You, God? It does seem like an impossible feat, doesn't it? I mean, God is perfect and man is so imperfect, who could ever live with someone like God?

God answers David's questions using three ideas: they must live honestly, practice righteousness,

Being a person of character and integrity is a choice.

and acknowledge truth. All three of these actions speak of a person's character. The person God describes is honest; lives right; and they recognize, speak, and love the truth. These people have integrity.

Being a person of character and integrity is a choice. Believers can choose to be people of character and integrity or choose not to be. Unbelievers can choose the same. It isn't automatic with either believers or unbelievers. I know lots of professing Christians with whom I would never want to do business because they lack integrity and character.

On the other hand, I know people who have never attended a church in their life, whom I would completely trust in a business transaction. They have integrity. They are honest.

A close friend of mine recently contacted a well-known, highly respected pastor in the state where I live. My friend had firsthand knowledge of a situation that had occurred a month or so earlier and called the pastor to ask him about his role in the matter. Unaware that my friend knew about the whole ordeal, he began to put a spin on the story that left the pastor in a much more favorable light, and in a position where he wouldn't be held accountable for his part in the incident. When my friend let him know that he knew what had really occurred, the pastor immediately changed his story. Unfortunately when the pastor got the call he didn't know my friend wasn't calling to check for information's sake, he was calling for integrity's sake.

Sadly, he blew it. In a moment, caught between a rock and a hard place, unaware that he would be discovered, he chose to protect his image rather than his integrity. When we find ourselves on the spot, so to speak, it's hard to maintain both. We are forced to make a decision, and if we aren't careful, we will choose just as poorly as this pastor.

For the record, please understand, this pastor is a good man. He typically is a man of integrity and character. He is a gifted man who is used of God mightily, but on this occasion he chose not to demonstrate those qualities. I've made the same kind of bad choices on occasion. I don't want to appear to be too hard on him, but I do want to emphasize that even good men, men with impeccable records, have to make choices. Integrity is earned daily. Maintaining integrity requires one to constantly make difficult, right choices.

> *Maintaining integrity requires one to constantly make difficult, right choices.*

Verse 3 of this Psalm also indicates that the person who can live with God does not slander, harm, or discredit his neighbor. The assault on one's neighbor that David has in mind here, doesn't appear to be physical but verbal. The offender harms his neighbor by telling a lie about him or by spreading a harmful rumor.

Again, these kinds of actions reflect on one's character and integrity. They are not representative of God's character. The one who does these things chooses to act in this fashion. We can't plea that they just crept out of our mouth unaware. We are very aware of what comes out of our mouths. We can stop, or we can carelessly continue.

My son recently told me of a conversation he had with his sister regarding my mother, who had passed away about two months earlier. He said Angela told him that in spite of her sadness over my mother's passing, she had absolutely no regrets in regard to my mom ("Ma" as she was known by all of us). "Ma never said a word to me for which she had to apologize, and I never spoke a word to her for which I needed to apologize," my daughter, told him. Matthew said, "Dad, that's how it was with me too." I told him, "Son, that's how it was with me and her as well. I'm sure as a boy I said things for which I needed to apologize, but since I left home at eighteen, I never remember saying anything to my mom for which I was ashamed and she most certainly never said anything hurtful to me."

Now lest you think we are all a bunch of angels, let me tell you, none of us could say that about each other or hardly anyone else we've known very long. Angela and Matthew both have pretty good filters, but I'm more of a "speak, think, apologize" guy. But my mom—wow!—she was always careful when she opened her mouth. She knew her tongue could be a vicious weapon if allowed to speak unharnessed by love and kindness. Like few I've ever met, my mom had control of her tongue almost all the time. She measured her words. How did she do that? Super Christian? No, she simply exercised her right to make a choice!

Verse 4 of Psalm 15 gives us even greater insight into the matter of who may live with God. This person judges other people on the basis of their love and obedience to God, rather than on the standard employed by the world in evaluating men.

Our world determines people's value on the basis of their credit score, appearance on the society page, number of trophies won or honors bestowed, academic degrees held, or even their address. But attention paid to how we honor God? Yeah, right.

Additionally, the person who can live with God speaks the truth, he doesn't lie. The King James Version uses a phrase we no longer employ in translating this verse, but I love it. It says, "He sweareth to his own hurt, and changeth not."

When my friend asked the question of the pastor, it wasn't a check on the facts, it was a check for integrity. In fact, let me give any teen who happens to be reading this book a heads up. Lots of time, when your folks, a teacher or a coach asks a question, they already know the answer. They aren't asking for information, they are checking to see if you have integrity.

If we aren't careful, we can talk ourselves into sacrificing integrity for image. "Man, I was in a jam. I didn't want to look like a goofball, so I had to make something up on the fly. I would have looked terrible if I had told the truth."

Really? And when you are caught in a lie, what image do you think that gave you? I promise you, even a flake looks better than a liar.

Finally, according to verse 5, the one who can live with God is not greedy, nor does he take advantage of another's weakness. He can't be bought. Can you? Keep in mind people sell out for more than just money. Sometimes it is popularity, promotion, or to avoid ridicule and harassment.

Success in life is aided by a number of qualities: knowledge, gift-edness, having a winsome personality, the ability to communicate one's thoughts and certainly enthusiasm, and effort. But all of those qualities fade quickly without integrity and character. Choose to be a man or woman of character. Choose to always demonstrate integrity; nothing will serve you better throughout your life.

QUESTIONS TO TALK ABOUT

1.   Someone has said, "character is what you demonstrate when no one is watching." How would you define or describe character and integrity?

2.   Who is someone you know who you think exemplifies character and integrity?

3.   Have you ever lost confidence in someone because they failed to demonstrate character or integrity?

4.   Have you ever been put on the spot, where telling the truth meant you would look foolish or be embarrassed? What did you do?

5.   Can a person regain integrity once lost?

CHAPTER TEN

CHOOSING MY ATTITUDE

ONE OF THE MOST CRITICAL choices you will ever make, in terms of determining how successful, joyful, and fulfilled a life you will live, is that of determining the attitude with which you will face life. Your attitude will greatly impact your happiness. It will determine how you respond to adversity, success, and every person you ever encounter. Maintaining a positive, healthy attitude is work; it requires making some conscious, intentional decisions.

So what impacts my attitude, anyway?

Some try to convince themselves it is predetermined. In the world of genetics, predestination

> *Your attitude will greatly impact your happiness.*

is a non-debatable reality. If my father is five foot nothing, the likelihood of me becoming an NBA center is remote. If, however, my mother attended Harvard, the likelihood of me getting into at least a decent college is probably pretty favorable. If my family has a history of mental illness, I need to face the reality that I may not be exempt either. One's ancestry isn't always a road map of knowing where one is headed physically, mentally, or emotionally, but it often gives us a hint as to what may be in store for future generations.

By the same token, temperamental traits can be passed on from one family member to another. These traits may not be as much about genetics, however, as environment. If I have lived with a whiner, I will naturally learn to whine. It's a behavior I have witnessed again and again since I was a child. In fact, I will probably think it is rather normal behavior. However, if I live with Pollyanna, the chances are also good that I will have learned to be cheerful and positive.

But here is a wonderful difference: if I inherit my father's protruding nose, I may not be able to do anything about that unless I consult a plastic surgeon. However if I nag and complain because I grew up in that kind of environment, I can change that behavior. It is a choice and it certainly is a difficult one to make, but it's a choice, nonetheless.

Not only do genetics and environment play a role in determining the attitude I demonstrate in life, but my circumstances play a role as well. Pretty easy to be cheery and bright when you have a great job, lots of money, good health, well-behaved children and everybody sings your praises. But lose a job, have debt collectors hounding you about your house payment, get called to the principal's office because your son showed the girls in PE class the tattoo he just got on his rear, and it's a lot tougher to be Mr. Sunshine. Circumstances impact attitude

We always have a choice—always.

for sure, but they don't *determine* attitude—ever.

While attitude is *affected* by temperament, environment, and circumstance, it is *determined* only by *choice*. We always have a choice—always. We convince ourselves otherwise at times, but in reality it is always a choice. The first three factors flavor our choice; they set the stage for our choice, but they don't determine it. And, for sure, this is not just "take responsibility for your actions" cheerleading propaganda. It is based on cold, hard, irrefutable, proven facts.

Think of all the people you know who had fathers or mothers with the disposition of a porcupine, that you found to be gracious, likeable, and kind. Think of those you know who lived in homes where all they received was criticism and negativity, and yet were constantly upbeat and positive. And, perhaps most telling, those who you knew who were poor, in horrible health, had every reason on earth to complain but never had anything but kind, positive things to say about life—who viewed themselves as being eternally blessed.

I've known bunches and bunches of people who fall in that category.

Elsie Hartline is one of the finest examples I ever knew. Mrs. Hartline lost her husband to suicide the first year I was her pastor. She had developed the worst case of Rheumatoid Arthritis I have ever encountered. Her hands were so terribly twisted and gnarled from the arthritis that you could not imagine how she could even tolerate the pain. In spite of that, she never missed church, constantly smiled, and always encouraged her family and friends for any little thing they did.

I could literally spend the next 100 pages telling of people whose stories are like those of Mrs. Hartline—people who received more than their share of heartache, but who chose to demonstrate positive attitudes toward life. Unfortunately, I've also encountered lots of others whose circumstances were the polar opposite of those I've just mentioned—people who never found time to do anything but complain and demonstrate bitterness. If you want to be bitter, negative and resentful in life, I assure you, it won't take much heartache for you to do it and feel justified in your choice. It will come easy. No hard choice to make there. But you can choose, in spite of your background, in spite of your circumstances, in spite of your temperament, to be happy, pleasant, and a joy to others. The choice is yours.

So how about it? What do you choose?

Let's say you are poor. Know any rich people who are miserable? Money must not be the answer.

Have a serious, life-threatening disease? Know any healthy, robust people who aren't happy? Sure you do; the woods are full of them. We don't even miss health until it's gone, but it didn't make us happy when we had it. The lack of good health can only make an unhappy person *more unhappy*.

Let's say you are just a sour puss. You complain, find fault, and constantly criticize those around you. And, you are quick to share how you've never gotten a fair shake in life. If things were to change for you, what would have to happen? Is the world going to change for you? Of all the people on earth, you know it's not. So what must happen if you ever want to be someone different than who you are? *You have to change.* You must choose to stop thinking, feeling, and acting as though you are a victim. You constantly say, "No one cares." You are right! So stop complaining. It hasn't changed anything to this point in time, why would it change anything in the future? Stop it! Make the right choice. I will stop complaining. I will stop criticizing anybody about anything! I will smile. I will learn to say, "Oh, I'm fine. And you?"

Now I know there are lots of psychologists and talk show hosts who will tell you not to mask your feelings. For lots of people, that's good advice. Not for you though. You constantly apprise people of how you feel and they hate you for it. So do yourself a huge favor, stop it!

The Apostle Paul gave some seriously good advice when he wrote from prison the words recorded in Philippians 4:

> Rejoice in the Lord always. I will say it again: Rejoice! Let your graciousness be known to everyone . . . whatever is true, whatever is honorable, whatever is just, whatever is pure, whatever is lovely, whatever is commendable—if there is any moral excellence and if there is any praise—dwell on these things . . . for I have learned to be content in whatever circumstances I am. I know both how to have a little, and I know how to have a lot. In any and all circumstances I have learned the secret of being content—whether well fed or hungry, whether in abundance or in need. (Phil. 4:4-5a, 8, 11b-12)

Do yourself a favor, take Paul's advice!

QUESTIONS TO TALK ABOUT

1.   In your case, do you believe your attitude is determined more by choice, circumstances, DNA, environment, or something else?

2.   To which of the Pooh characters would your family and friends compare your attitude, if promised anonymity? A. Tigger B. Piglet C. Rabbit D. Eeyore E. Winnie the Pooh

3.   What about your attitude do you wish was different?

4.   For that change to occur, what choices would you have to consciously make?

5.   Complete the following sentence: For the next twenty-four hours I choose to be more/less _____ _____ in an effort to improve my attitude. In order to make that happen, I will: _____ _____.

CHAPTER ELEVEN

CHOOSING TO BE SECURE AND CONFIDENT

THERE ARE PEOPLE IN LIFE who appeal to virtually all of us. They come from a wide range of backgrounds. Some are pretty people, but others aren't. Some are smart, others, not so much. Some are athletic, while some are a little clumsy. Some are wealthy, but others are a couple of dollars from being broke. Some, like myself are a little redneck, and others are blue bloods. But regardless of their status, they have appeal. We like them. They make us feel good to be in their presence.

And then there the people we try, almost universally, to avoid. They too come in all shapes and sizes. So what's the difference in the two groups?

It has virtually nothing to do with appearance, standing, money, abilities, or education—the things we so often tout as being the determiners of success.

It's all about how they view themselves. People we find attractive are almost always secure and confident. Because they are comfortable with themselves, we are comfortable with them as well. They aren't cocky, they don't have to be. They aren't braggarts, and they are secure. They know they aren't perfect, but they are okay with that.

On the other hand, people plagued with insecurities, who lack confidence, are almost always high maintenance, which frankly, makes people steer clear of them.

The Bible gives us clear-cut examples of both types. Even more importantly, it admonishes us to live secure, confident lives.

Let's begin by taking a look at a few of the examples the Bible gives us of insecure people. The first murder ever committed was an example of domestic violence. Abel made an offering to God that was found acceptable and pleasing to the Lord. When his brother Cain attempted to do the same, his offering was rejected. Instead of remedying the situation, Cain, in anger and jealousy, killed his brother.

In 1 Kings 19, Elijah, one of the boldest preachers to ever live, loses heart because of a threat made against him by Jezebel and runs for his life. In exhaustion, he falls down and asks God to let him die. He is convinced all is lost and that he is the only one who really loves and serves God any longer.

What about King Saul? He may be the worst of the bunch when it comes to insecurity. David, as a teenage boy, rescues Israel during his reign by mustering the courage to go to battle with Goliath. Instead of demonstrating gratitude, Saul becomes jealous as they return home because the women come out into the streets and sing "Saul has slain his thousands, but David his tens of thousands." Saul hadn't actually slain thousands, and David certainly hadn't slain tens of thousands. In fact, David had only managed at this point to kill one man—Goliath. The women were in the streets celebrating Israel's victory, just as they should have been. They were showing appreciation to both Saul for his leadership and David for his courage. It must have been a pretty funny sight, seeing them return from battle. Saul, the Bible notes, was a very tall man. David, on the other hand, was something of a runt at this age. It must have looked like Mutt and Jeff returning from war. How could a grown man—a king no less—be jealous of a young boy who has just proven his loyalty so dramatically? In his insanity, Saul tries, on multiple occasions to pin David to the wall with his spear.

And talk about insecurity, get a load of Herod when the Wise Men visit him. He is so insecure, when they fail to return to report the Messiah's location following his birth, he issues a decree that all the male children in the region up to two years of age be put to death. Afraid of a baby? He can't possibly become a threat for at least twenty-five years! But sadly, insecurity isn't rational. It's a dangerous form of emotional illness.

> *. . . insecurity isn't rational. It's a dangerous form of emotional illness.*

Thankfully, the Bible also gives us a picture of what it looks like to be secure in one's manhood. Take a look at Noah. Talk about secure. This guy builds a ship, 450 feet long, in the middle of nowhere. Why? Because God told him to do so. God said it was going to rain. Noah believed him, but no one else did. Day after day for eighty years or longer they must have come by and taunted old Noah.

"Whatcha doin' Noah?"

"Buildin' an ark."

"A what?"

"An ark. A boat."

"But Noah, there's no water around here?"

"There will be!"

"Noah, you are a nutcase!"

I can hardly imagine the ribbing that Noah took until the day the rain began to fall. There isn't the slightest hint, however, that Noah ever wavered. Why? He was secure in what he believed, in what he knew he had heard God say. It didn't matter what those on the outside were saying. All that mattered is what Noah knew in his heart.

In fact, the Bible is replete with examples of secure men and women, acting confidently as they are convinced that God is leading them to act—Moses, Joshua, Caleb, Daniel, Ezra, Nehemiah, Esther, Deborah, John the Baptist, and Jesus as He stands before Pilate. Wow! What a picture of someone demonstrating what it means to be secure! What are some of the lessons we learn from these characters about being both secure and insecure?

For openers, insecure people believe that everything said or done, in spite of how remote the connection, was aimed at hurting them and that it was intentional. Secure people are more thick-skinned than that. Remember the example I cited in regard to Saul in 1 Samuel 18:6-9? "Saul hath slain his thousands, but David his ten thousands." That wasn't meant to defame Saul; to the contrary, it was a compliment to both he and David. But, he took it that way, and my experience with insecure people leads me to believe that you could have never convinced Saul otherwise. Insecurity isn't rational.

Secure people don't have to be in the limelight. They don't always have to be praised for everything they do. It is enough for them to know they did something worthwhile. John the Baptist provides us with one of the best examples of this you will ever find. Take a look at John 3:25-30:

> Then a dispute arose between John's disciples and a Jew about purification. So they came to John and told him, "Rabbi, the One you testified about, and who was with you across the Jordan, is baptizing—and everybody is flocking to Him."
>
> John responded, "No one can receive a single thing unless it's given to him from heaven. You yourselves can testify that I said, 'I am not the Messiah, but I've been sent ahead of Him.' He who has the bride is the groom. But the groom's friend, who stands by

and listens for him, rejoices greatly at the groom's voice. So this joy of mine is complete. He must increase, but I must decrease."

John knew that his was a secondary role. But he also recognized that there was great honor in even being in a secondary role. Honor comes not in being the biggest name on the marquee, but rather in being given a task to do and doing it well.

Secure people are internally driven instead of externally driven. They judge themselves on the basis of what they know to be true about themselves and not on the basis of what others say, positively or negatively.

Think about Moses for a moment. He received criticism from everybody! He caught it from his people, his wife, his father- in-law, Pharaoh, Aaron, and Miriam. The only two who weren't critical of him were Caleb and Joshua. But the criticism never greatly impacted his actions.

But here is the mark of really being secure. Moses likewise wasn't overly impressed by the compliments that people no doubt paid him. Can you imagine what they must have said about him when he parted the Red Sea or returned from the mountain with his face aglow because he had been in the presence of God? The Bible says that Moses was the most humble man who ever lived. Most preachers I know, including this one, would have an ego the size of Texas if we did a tenth of what Moses did.

Do you covet the praise and acceptance of men, rather than finding satisfaction in knowing you have acted as you should?

And finally, always keep in mind that **anyone, at any given time, is capable of behaving securely or insecurely**. Know what Elijah, Peter, Moses, and Abraham have in common? All of them are seen in the scripture at one time or another as examples of what it is to live both securely and insecurely. Realize even though you may typically be one or the other, you are capable of both.

No one, knowingly, wants to be insecure. So how do I avoid that? Here are a few choices you need to make.

Choose not to be quick to take offense. People can and do say stupid things, sometimes intentionally but often times unintentionally. People have bad days, when they say things they later regret. People can make you their scapegoat. One thing I hate about our country is how thin skinned we have become. Some folks are just way too sensitive. In fact, if you pride yourself in being sensitive to others, beware. Those who are overly sensitive to others typically are overly sensitive about comments directed toward themselves as well.

Choose to judge yourself by God's standards and not man's. When God told Samuel to go to Jesse and anoint one of his sons as king, Samuel thought surely it would be the eldest son. But listen to what God told him in 1 Samuel 16:7:

> But the Lord said to Samuel, "Do not look at his appearance or his stature, because I have rejected him. Man does not see what the Lord sees, for man sees what is visible, but the Lord sees the heart."

Choose to remember you are the work of God, physically, mentally and spiritually.

Psalm 139: 13-14, 16 says:

> For it was You who created my inward parts; You knit me together in my mother's womb. I will praise You because I have been remarkably and wonderfully made. Your works are wonderful, and I know this very well. Your eyes saw me when I was formless; all my days were written in Your book and planned before a single one of them began.

Paul tells us that as believers we are a work in progress. Ephesians 2:10 says,

For we are His creation, created in Christ Jesus for good works,
which God prepared ahead of time so that we should walk in them.

The word for creation, transliterated from Greek to English is "poem." We are God's poem—His creative expression. It is hard for me to imagine that in Him, as we surrender ourselves to Him, we are not exactly what He wants us to be. There is no room for insecurity in the life of a believer who is walking with God.

Finally, choose to believe that in Christ you are sufficient for any task He asks you to undertake.

I am able to do all things through Him who strengthens me. (Phil. 4:13)

Christians ought to be the most humble, yet confident, secure people on the planet. We shouldn't be angry or threatened by those who would attempt to undermine us. Our hope is in Christ. He wants you to live victoriously. Choose to do that today.

> *He wants you to live victoriously. Choose to do that today.*

QUESTIONS TO TALK ABOUT

1. Can you still recall a time when someone said something to you as a child that robbed you of your confidence?

2. Who is one of the most secure, non-threatened human beings you know?

3. If you struggle with being secure, are you aware of what feeds your insecurity?

4. What would you have to do to become more secure?

5. Do you think that talking with a counselor might help you uncover the source of your insecurity and put it behind you?

CHAPTER TWELVE

CHOOSING TO BE LESS ANGRY AND ANGRY LESS

I REMEMBER THE FIRST TIME I was ever given Novocain. I thought, *wow, this is the coolest drug I've ever seen.* You can't feel any pain. But then someone said, "Pain is your friend." I thought that sounded crazy, but then they went on to explain that pain is a warning signal to our bodies that something is wrong. It alerts us that we have a problem. If I couldn't feel pain, I might inadvertently lay my hand on something extremely hot that would badly burn me. Pain enables me at the very outset to know I am being burned. So while no one likes to feel pain, pain really isn't our enemy; it's our friend.

No one who wants to live for God and likes getting along with others, likes to feel anger. But anger, like pain, isn't our enemy. Anger is a warning system. It sometimes alerts us that we are about to be tempted to lose it, and it tells us that we have a problem—that there is something not to our liking. The trick is to figure out what the problem is, rather than act on the anger. But anger, in and of itself, isn't a bad emotion.

Some people have a high threshold for pain—most of them

Anger is a warning system.

are female. Men typically fall more into the weenie category. Equally unimpressive, is the fact that men typically have less tolerance for anger than do women. While some men can handle a great deal of anger before it begins to show, others fly off the handle at a moment's notice.

Sadly, some aren't even embarrassed by their outbursts—stupidly, a few even believe it's actually a sign that they are really a man.

The key, is to recognize that we are angry, understand why, and respond in a healthy way.

How do we learn to deal with our anger? *The key, is to recognize that we are angry, understand why we are angry and respond to our anger in a healthy way.*

Let's take a look at six biblical examples of people experiencing anger. Three of these are examples of anger leading to inappropriate action. The other three of these examples, believe it or not, are examples of anger being dealt with righteously, which proves you can be angry and not sin.

The first is Cain. He becomes enraged when God accepts his brother, Abel's offering but refuses to accept his. The end result, he kills his own brother.

Then there's the case of Joseph's brothers. In a jealous rage that had been brewing for some time because of their father's foolish preferential treatment of Joseph, they decide in a moment of passion to sell him into slavery. They had first intended to kill him but seized the opportunity to cash in on their brother's demise instead.

Through a wild turn of events the descendants of Joseph and his brothers find themselves in slavery in Egypt 430 years later. When God sends Moses to secure their release, they are less than thrilled with his leadership, despite how many times Moses proves to be exactly what the doctor ordered. In fact, their complaining becomes so vocal at one point, Moses is fearful they are about to stone him to death. Why were they so angry? They were afraid. They are constantly fearful that they have been led into the desert to die. In their minds they would have been better off back in Egypt.

Now if you haven't read these, the next two examples of anger are going to surprise you. Jesus! Bet you didn't see that coming.

Yes, Jesus, is the center of two examples of anger. First when Jesus learns that His disciples are turning away children and their parents, the bible says He became indignant.

And then, not once, but twice, at the beginning and again at the end of His ministry, Jesus goes ballistic in the Temple. According to the scripture, He constructs a whip and enters the area turning over tables and flailing away at the money changers. It would have been a sight to see! In South Carolina we would have said, "He gave 'em a whoopin'."

Does it seem over the top? For us? Yes, yes it does. Try doing that today and you would be arrested and rightfully so. But not for Him. His judgment is perfect; He judged them as God. You and I are never free to break the law of the land. We need to leave punishment in the hands of God and the courts. But Jesus, He was absolutely right to act as He did.

And the last example, though there are numerous others I could cite, is that of Paul. Paul got mad on several occasions, but the reason I have chosen Paul is because of the one with whom he is angry. Paul gets put out with Peter, the clear leader of the early church. Why? Because he sees Peter act in a two-faced fashion. Peter, Paul, Barnabas, and all the Gentile believers are having a wonderful time of fellowship in Antioch until some Jewish believers from Jerusalem show up, and Peter politely distances himself from his Gentile friends. Paul gets chapped about it. Paul calls Peter out—publicly!

But what is equally impressive is that he didn't stop speaking to him, ministering with him, or make more of it than he should have. He called his hand, corrected the problem and moved on. He straightened the whole mess out before it could fester and create a real problem for the church. In short, he handled it like a Christian.

Like it or not, you are going to get angry. God has wired you that way. If you want to act appropriately when you feel anger, you must do three things.

Recognize you are angry. In the biblical case studies I just cited, there is no evidence that either Cain or the Hebrew people recognized they were angry. They simply acted on their anger. In the one case, Cain was hurt that his offering had been rejected. He probably felt embarrassed. With the Hebrews they felt fearful. They were afraid they were going to die. Instinctively, they directed their anger toward the one who was their leader. They blamed Moses for all the problems they encountered along the way.

Jesus, however, realizes He is angry in both incidents I cited. He realizes His disciples have overstepped their bounds. They have acted in a human fashion to a spiritual problem. They reasoned as human beings, that Jesus is important and doesn't have time to bless children. They think this is beneath Him, and it's not a good use of His time.

In the story of the cleansing of the Temple, Jesus sees the problem first, goes away to contemplate His next action, makes a whip, and returns to cleanse the Temple. He realized He was angry and prepared to take appropriate action.

Likewise Paul directs his anger at the problem. It isn't that he dislikes Peter but rather that he recognizes that Peter has acted hypocritically, and it is harming others. Paul calls Peter out for it.

But we must do more than recognize we are angry. We must determine why we are angry.

We can become angry for a multitude of reasons. It can be due to fear, jealousy, embarrassment, selfishness. Maybe it's that you aren't getting your way, insecurity, an inability to control people or circumstances, or you simply have a difference of preference. It may be for righteous reasons such as inequity, mistreatment or cruelty to others, or someone taking advantage of the weak and helpless.

But be sure of this, **you are a long way toward responding appropriately if you understand the real reason for your anger**.

Years ago I was working on an advanced degree and it required me to take a semester of CPE (Clinical Pastoral Education). I went to Winston-Salem and took the course at the Baptist Hospital, which was a part of the Bowman Gray School of Medicine. During the course we had to participate in IPR (Interpersonal Relationships). It was basically a time when you reflected over your life and tried to deal with all the baggage you had acquired to that point. One of the things I discovered about myself was that I could be smiling on the outside and be angry on the inside. They told me that feeling is pretty much par for the course for a lot of us pastors. We learn to veil our anger because we have a fear that if we let people know we are angry it will cause problems or we won't seem very Christ-like.

So one of the things they told us to do is to identify when we felt ourselves getting angry and to tell someone how we felt.

One Sunday morning, after having waxed eloquent, I am standing at the front door of the church greeting worshippers, and this lady comes out who rubbed me the wrong way just about every time I was around her. She was a nice lady and just always wanted to tell me how they used to do things in the mega church in Florida where she had been a member before coming to our little hick town. Even more of a problem to me was the fact that she was always so serious. We never had what most people would consider an ordinary conversation. It was always about the "deep things of God."

Well, she shakes my hand, is pleasant enough, but then she begins a conversation that I can tell is going to be both lengthy and extremely serious, something no preacher wants to have after talking all morning. I let her talk for about two minutes and then, out of nowhere, almost beyond my control, like Captain Marvel in Wonder Comics— Shazaam!—I said it. I went where pastors are not suppose to go. I told her what I was feeling. (I will never forget the look of wonder on my wife's face as she stood speechless beside me, staring at me as though aliens from outer space had taken possession of my body.) "Mrs. So-and-so, it's strange, but I feel myself getting angry as you talk," I said.

The look of bewilderment on her face was priceless! My first thought was, "Oh, heck! There's no going back now!" She said with a look of disbelief, "What did I say to make you angry?" To which I responded, "I don't know. Let me think about it."

Then, after about a five second delay, I said as kindly as I could, "I think it's that you never ever ask me about the weather, or the Clemson Tigers, or how my dog's doing." She looked absolutely stunned, so I continued while I was on a roll. "It's that you always want to ask me about serious stuff and never seem interested in me." She turned and walked out—and though she never said—I think she was pretty mad. She never came back. And, we all lived happily ever after!

The final part of dealing with anger is to **respond to it in a healthy way.**

Having recognized your anger, and having evaluated your reason for being angry, whenever possible, *let it go*. If it is unjustifiable or if you have transferred your anger about some circumstance to someone who really isn't to blame, let it go. If it is an inappropriate reason to be angry, let it go. An example of this would be that you prefer one thing and someone else prefers something else. A difference in preference isn't a sign of moral superiority. Other examples of anger to let go would be anger you feel because you are merely embarrassed, insecure, or aren't getting your way. In fact, most times, let it go.

Recognize that you have a choice. Even when anger is justified, you can choose to let it go. You can exercise forgiveness. You can choose to suffer insult and injury. Jesus did for your sake. Why couldn't you? You can take the high road. Always be aware of what James said:

> For man's anger does not accomplish God's righteousness.
> *(James 1:20)*

Can you act in righteous indignation and not sin? Yes. Are the odds in your favor? No. You likely will go too far, say too much, and be too harsh.

And when you do act on your anger, make sure you always act appropriately. Even if my anger is justified, is the level of my anger appropriate? Even when it comes to war, our military leaders have standards they use to answer the question, "Is this a just war?" You ought to have some standard of measurement as well.

- Ever seen road rage that was entirely beyond any kind of reasonable reaction? We all have.

- Ever heard yourself ranting at your spouse or children in a way, in view of their mistake, that was absolutely nuts?

- Ever got into an argument that started out appropriately enough as an expression of varying opinions that escalated into something of a crime scene?

If you are someone who finds yourself expressing your anger in a fashion like that I have just mentioned, you need to take a class in anger management. In addition to typical anger management classes, Celebrate Recovery is available in a growing number of towns and cities across America. It isn't only for anger management, but is a program designed to help people deal with every hurt, habit, and hang-up that keeps people from being the person they want to be.

Others of you aren't criminal with your anger but you are constantly getting into to it with people unnecessarily. Stop damaging relationships by having an uncontrolled temper. Make a choice. Do something about your anger today! Controlling your temper will change your life for the better. It will keep you from looking stupid. It will protect your testimony. It will improve your relationship with your family and friends. You can choose to make a change. Do it today.

QUESTIONS TO TALK ABOUT

1. Do you think you always demonstrate the appropriate degree of anger when someone does something while driving that angers you?

2. Have you ever been embarrassed by your failure to control your temper?

3. What are some things you do to help curb your anger?

4. How does it make you feel when someone is expressing strong anger toward you?

CHAPTER THIRTEEN

CHOOSING TO NOT BE CONTROLLED BY OTHERS

OR
MOVE OVER, BUCKO, I'M DRIVING THIS BUS!

EVERY WAKING MOMENT THERE ARE people endeavoring to influence how you think and what you do. They desire nothing less than to control you. Some of you are thinking, this guy is paranoid. I don't think so. They want to influence how we dress, which colors we prefer, what college to attend, which phone you buy, the candidates you elect, and the food you eat.

> *We can't really escape the attempt to influence us; what we can do is recognize the attempt and determine for ourselves whether that is a direction we want to go.*

There are many people out there who even want you to feel about what happens in the world, the same way they feel about it. They don't just report the news any more, they influence it and at times, they make it.

In fairness, it's not just the advertisers, manufacturers, and news agencies who want to manipulate your choices. Many people are trying to influence you because they love you or because they think they know what is best for you. Parents, teachers, coaches, pastors, friends, and enemies—lots of folk—want to impact your decisions. We can't really escape the attempt to influence us; what we can do is recognize the attempt and determine for ourselves whether that is a direction we want to go.

Consider the following biblical characters and see if you can determine what influenced them to act as they did.

Let's start with Eve. Remember what impacted her decision to disobey God?

What about Adam? He just blindly followed Eve, didn't he?

Samson? He had a problem with women; he couldn't say no to a pretty face.

No human was said to be wiser than Solomon. So what changed his thinking?

King Ahab, the king of Israel, at one point was as wicked as they come, but he was also something of a weasel. Remember what influenced him to be as aggressive as he was?

Then there is King Herod who beheaded John the Baptist. The Bible says he actually didn't want to kill John. So why did he?

Why would Bathsheba, married to a good man, sleep with David, a man she apparently didn't even know?

And one final character—Pilate. Pilate had Jesus executed after he found Him innocent. Pilate pleaded with the crowd to release Jesus because of His innocence but in the end gave the order to have Him scourged and crucified. What influenced Pilate's decision?

> *. . . every time we make a bad decision, it's ours, no matter who or what the influence might have been.*

Sometimes we make bad decisions completely on our own. Often times, however, it is due in large part to the influence of others. To be sure—every time we make a bad decision, it's ours, no matter who or what the influence might have been.

So what were the strategies employed to get people to act against their will?

In the case of Adam, Solomon, Bathsheba, and Pilate, it was *a desire to please others*. Adam wanted to please Eve. Solomon adopted idolatrous practices to please his many wives. Bathsheba wanted to please a handsome, powerful king. Pilate wanted to please Rome. Rome didn't want to hear of the "goings on" of Jerusalem, they wanted peace, so why make waves over an innocent Jew losing his life?

It's amazing how many of us will forfeit our own desires, ambitions, dreams, and even conscience in order to avoid saying no to those we want to please. The desire to please can lead to our success, but it can also lead to a loss of our identity, character, and dreams. Be careful about becoming a people pleaser.

A desire to gain sexual favors influenced Samson, Herod, and, literally, millions of others. One of the most successful and talented men I have ever known said, "In America, if a man can keep his pants on, the sky is the limit." That's a mighty big "if." We've all known lots of good men and women whose careers and, more importantly, lives, were sabotaged by an inability to control their sexual appetite.

Affairs are a choice. Using pornography is a choice. Acting sexually inappropriate is a choice. They are all choices with bitter consequences. At stake is often a man or woman's family, children, reputation, career, and self-image. It's a choice that isn't worth the pain that accompanies it.

A desire for fame and sophistication leads many to do foolish things. In fact, I believe that Solomon's desire for fame was even greater than his desire to please his wives. People traveled the world over to seek an audience with Solomon, and they brought all kinds of gifts. When you read of Solomon's provisions in 1 Kings 4, you are taken aback by all the excesses and extravagances of his life. He became a bigger than life figure in his own eyes. Think about it for a moment. Why would a man have 1,000 wives? He couldn't have even known all their names. It wasn't even about the sex; it was about his larger than life image. He had a need to prove he was the greatest man alive. But few were as miserable as Solomon according to his own memoirs in Ecclesiastes.

Some succumb to pressure because they are fearful of looking weak. Herod was just such a man. He allowed his mouth to overload his brain, and he promised his step-daughter the moon and the stars. When time came to pay off he couldn't believe she would be so crass as to ask for John's head on a platter. But he'd been played. Rather than back away from his oath in the company of all his friends, he went through this vile ordeal.

Some might ask, what could he have done, in view of the fact that he was such a powerful figure? He would have looked weak to back out now. Here is an important lesson in life to remember: regardless of who you are, *it's never too late to do the right thing.* Herod should have said, "Whoa! Man, I spoke too soon. I acted foolishly in writing you a blank check. I refuse to continue to act foolishly by fulfilling an unwise vow. I can't take the life of an innocent man for your mother's amusement. It's not going to happen." Weak? I don't think so. I have a feeling he might have gained some admirers that night had he acted in that fashion. As it was, his guests probably left disgusted and wondering what kind of hands the government of Israel was in.

Lastly, **some fold under the pressure of powerful people**. Bathsheba and Ahab both fall into that category. It is amazing how much sway people of influence can have over people who hold them in high regard. If we are not careful we can find ourselves doing things that we really don't want to do because of the request of a boss, parent, sibling, child, grandchild, spouse, or even a pastor or priest. Keep in mind, if this person respects you for who you are, they will likewise respect your refusal to comply with their wishes. Listen to those who give you advice when you know they have your best interest at heart, but never compromise your values to comply with the wishes of anyone. Just imagine this: what if when Bathsheba was taken to David's palace and he began to come on to her, she had looked him squarely in the eye and said, "David, you surprise me. I thought you were a better man than this. My husband, Uriah, is at this moment on the front line, protecting your kingdom. How dare you even consider such a thing?" It would have taken a lot of courage to conquer her apprehension and fear, but I promise you, knowing David to be the man that he was, he would have sent her home, repented of his sin and begged her forgiveness. But what's more, she wouldn't have become pregnant. Uriah wouldn't have died, the baby wouldn't have died, and David would have avoided great heartache. Choices matter. Sadly, Bathsheba and David made bad ones.

WHAT CAN I DO TO KEEP FROM BEING CONTROLLED BY OTHERS?

Know how God wants you to live. God has a plan for your life that will differ in some respects from the plan He has for others. But there are aspects of His will that are common for all men. There are moral absolutes given in the Word of God that neither vary from one culture to another nor change with the passing of time. You can only live as God expects you to live when you are a serious student of the scripture. How can you make the choices you should unless you know how God would have you live?

Decide who you are and where you believe He wants you to go with your life. Don't let others tell you who you are. Determine that for yourself. There are a number of biblical characters that indicate that God had a particular plan for their lives even before they were born. I believe we were all created to bring Him glory but I believe He intends to do that by having us do a wide variety of things with our lives. As surely as He intended that I should be a pastor, He intends that another be a brick mason, school teacher, or stay-at-home mom or dad. It isn't an easy task but each of us must determine who we are and what His specific will for our lives is. Don't settle for being a doctor or lawyer, as wonderful a career choice as either of those would be, if you believe He has created you to be a farmer. Contentment comes in knowing that you are in the center of God's will for your life.

Be willing to be the odd man out. Be your own person. Don't adopt the habits of the crowd. A few years back virtually every middle school and high school girl I met used the word "like," like all the time, man. There were times I thought I'd scream. It is so refreshing when you see a kid who isn't afraid to be his or her own person. We had a kid a few years back named Zeb Chamlee. He was just such a kid. You never forget that kind of kid. They stand out in the crowd. They have personality, are independent thinkers, and are so cool. Zeb would go to Good Will, before it was cool, and come back with a bowling shirt that he would wear to school. He and his sister, Sarah, were both fiercely independent. By the time they finished high school, they had hiked portions of the Appalachian Trail with just another friend. They are great young adults today. They didn't just turn out that way. Their parents helped them to achieve independence at an early age. We baby our kids too long and then wonder why they have difficulty standing on their own two feet and being independent.

Listen to advice and wisdom of others, but don't let others set the course for you. Be true to yourself. Don't spend your life being miserable to please someone else.

Don't allow yourself to be manipulated and don't enable others to mess their lives up. Parents don't let your kids manipulate you into giving into their demands, whether they are five or twenty-five. Don't be shamed into doing what you know you shouldn't. Many parents, in the name of helping their children out, have made their kids cripples. Flee from anyone who begins a sentence with "If you loved me . . ." and the same goes for adult children. Don't let your parents rule your life. They had a chance to live their lives and you should have an opportunity to live yours. Be loyal, take care of them, but don't surrender your life to another, even if it's your parent.

Lastly, don't allow yourself to be pressured into doing anything you know is stupid, life threatening, could result in the loss of your good name, or bring embarrassment to you or your family. There is never dishonor in responding honorably. Think of the consequences of an action before you take it. It's too late once you pull the trigger. Think, pray, and contemplate the consequences, and act with caution. Though it may seem far-fetched, consider the worst case scenario.

QUESTIONS TO TALK ABOUT

1. Can you think of a product you purchased recently and you know it was because of the influence of advertising?

2. When is the last time you experienced peer pressure?

3. To whom is it hard for you to say no?

4. On a scale of 1 to 10, how much do you think you are a free thinker vs. a conformer?

5. If you could take more control of your life in any one area, what would that be?

CHAPTER FOURTEEN

CHOOSING TO BE CONTENT

REMEMBER THE GAME SHOW, "LET'S Make a Deal?" There were three doors, and you got to pick which door you wanted. Well, imagine that we have two doors, only instead of you having to guess, I'm going to tell you what's behind each door. Then you take the door you want. Ready?

Behind door number one is $10,000,000.

Behind door number two is a formula. The formula contains the secret to being content. Which door do you choose?

Call me a skeptic but I'm betting if you are honest, you chose door number one. Right? In fairness, I am sure I would have too!

But think about it for a moment. If door number two really would provide us with all we would ever want, what could door number one provide, that we didn't already have?

I know, I know, you are thinking that if I had door number one, I wouldn't want anything else either. Really? As much as I want to go with door number one, I've got to say, it would not be all I would ever want. We'd go buy a fancy house and a few fancy cars, and we'd vacation at some cool spots. Did I mention I would retire? But I just know, it wouldn't be enough. We would sell the houses in time and buy something else. We would trade the cars, probably sooner than we think. I would certainly have enough money to last me the rest of my life but satisfied? Not a chance!

I mean, think about it. We all know, through magazines and television, plenty of people who have more than $10,000,000 and aren't satisfied. They bounce from one marriage to another, they have scrapes with the law, and they often seem more miserable than the rest of us with less zeros on the end of our bank statement.

Remember Socrates, from philosophy 101? He said, "The wealthiest man in the world is the one who has learned to be content." Think about it, if a person truly is content, there is nothing he or she could possibly want. So how could anyone be wealthier than that? Satisfied means satisfied. I've got all I need. In fact, if I don't need anything and someone gives me something anyway, is it really a gift? Doesn't it fit the role of burden better than gift? Ever wanted to say to someone trying to pawn something off on you, "No, please, I'm good." What you were thinking is, "Man, don't make me take that home, I don't have room for it." Unneeded stuff just clutters our lives. Right?

So which do you want?

Why is it so hard to be content?

Listen to what Paul tells us in Philippians 4:10-13:

> I rejoiced in the Lord greatly that once again you renewed your care for me. You were, in fact, concerned about me but lacked opportunity to show it. I don't say this out of need, for I have learned to be content in whatever circumstances I am. I know both how to have a little, and I know how to have a lot. In any and all circumstances I have learned the secret of being content—whether well fed or hungry, whether in abundance or in need. I am able to do all things through Him who strengthens me.

May I make a few quick observations?

Contentment is learned.

No one is born content. Just take a look at babies. Need I say more? Contentment is, therefore, not a trait or temperament with which you are born—it is learned. Therefore, none of us get a pass. If we choose, we can all learn to be content. But, no one is automatically content.

How, then, is it learned? How is it developed?

Paul, unfortunately, doesn't specifically tell us in neatly organized points, but I think we can figure it out.

Go back with me a few verses to Philippians 4:4:

Rejoice in the Lord always. I will say it again: Rejoice!

"Chairo" (KIGH-roh), the word, translated "rejoice," is one Paul used nine times in this letter. It means to enjoy a state of gladness, happiness or well-being. He even admonishes the Philippians to constantly dwell in a state of gladness, happiness, or well-being. Does he really mean in every situation? Unquestionably. How do I know? He is in prison as he writes this letter. Can you think of a more difficult place on this earth from which to rejoice? You know as he pens these words he is keenly aware of his circumstance. So, even in prison, rejoice.

How do I do that? Would I be glad to be in prison, sick with cancer, at the graveside of a loved one, or out looking for a job? No, of course not. What I can be joyful about is that even in the midst of this circumstance, I have the Lord. He is going to work through this circumstance. He is ever with me. He is going to care for me and protect me.

Contented people are joyful people. They recognize how blessed they are even when things may not be going well. Do you view yourself as blessed?

Contented people are gracious people. Take a look at the next verse:

> *Let your graciousness be known to everyone. The Lord is near.*
> *(Phil. 4:5)*

To show grace is to be Christ like. Ephesians 2:8-9 clearly shows the importance of grace in the life of a believer.

> *For you are saved by grace through faith, and this is not from your-*
> *selves; it is God's gift – not from works, so that no one can boast.*

God saves and forgives us not because we merit forgiveness but because He is gracious. Being gracious requires someone to demonstrate love and forgiveness where it isn't merited. People who do that, are always more likely to be contented because they don't have scores to settle. They aren't angry.

Contented people have great confidence in God's ability and refuse to dwell on their worries. Take a look at Philippians 4:6-7:

> Don't worry about anything, but in everything, through prayer
> and petition with thanksgiving, let your requests be made
> known to God. And the peace of God, which surpasses every
> thought, will guard your hearts and minds in Christ Jesus.

Try this. Stop talking about problems that arise and start praying about them. Contentment comes to those who believe that God is taking care of them. When we turn to family and friends and tell them all about our troubles without first talking to God, what almost always happens is that they think of other things that could go wrong that we haven't even considered yet. And, let's face it—they typically aren't in a position to do anything

Stop talking about problems ... start praying about them.

to remedy the situation. God is! Why not tell Him everything before we tell others anything?

Contented people are thankful for what they have. The prayer he talks about isn't just asking God for what we need; it's thanking God for all He's done. Make a list of all the ways God has blessed you. When your heart is filled with thanksgiving, it's hard to focus on what you don't have and that's what discontentment is all about.

Contented people guard their minds and hearts. I love verse 8. In fact, it's why I never watch horror movies!

Finally, brothers, whatever is just, whatever is pure, whatever is lovely, whatever is commendable—if there is any moral excellence and if there is any praise—dwell on these things. (Phil. 4:8)

Paul admonishes us to not give into negative, corrupt, or unhealthy thinking. It's pretty easy to see that if people tend to think about all they don't have instead of all they do have, they are going to be pretty miserable campers. We become what we think. Think positively!

Contented people are focused on what really matters.

Do what you have learned and received and heard and seen in me, and the God of peace will be with you. (Phil 4:9)

What do we learn about Paul in reading the New Testament? What I am about to say will probably surprise you, but Paul wasn't a guy with whom most of us would have enjoyed hanging out. He wasn't your run of the mill, half-hearted Christian. He was a guy who was intense to the third power. Paul was focused like a laser on what mattered in life. And Paul promises if we imitate him, live as he lived, we WILL HAVE the peace of God. No questions asked. But it comes in being focused on the things of God, as he was focused on the things of God.

Listen to Paul's testimony in Philippians 3:7-11:

But everything that was a gain to me, I have considered to be a loss because of Christ. More than that, I also consider everything to be a loss in view of the surpassing value of knowing

> Christ Jesus my Lord. Because of Him I have suffered the loss
> of all things and consider them filth, so that I may gain Christ
> and be found in Him, not having a righteousness of my own
> from the law, but one that is through faith in Christ—the
> righteousness from God based on faith. My goal is to know
> Him and the power of His resurrection and the fellowship of
> His sufferings, being conformed to His death, assuming that
> I will somehow reach the resurrection from among the dead.

Paul never concerned himself with so many things that occupy us because they have no meaning in his life. If you are ever going to be content, the things of God will have to become more meaningful to you than anything else. If your chief concern is on the material, the temporal, and not the spiritual, you will always want—because there will always be something bigger, better and completely new.

Contented people have to experience some hard, difficult times. They have to have their "want" list shortened. Look at verse 12.

> I know both how to have a little, and I know how to have a lot.
> In any and all circumstances I have learned the secret of being
> content—whether well fed or hungry, whether in abundance
> or in need. (Phil. 4:12)

Virtually all of us have a "want list." When I was a kid the big deal was to get the Sear's or J.C. Penny Wish book. Every kid would go through their Christmas edition and circle in red the things they wanted for Christmas. You would typically change your mind a dozen times or more, so by the time Christmas rolled around, virtually everything had been circled or crossed out. The anticipation of getting something new was often better than the receiving of the gift itself.

Here's what's weird about "want lists:" it doesn't matter how long the want list might be, when significant difficulties arise, our "want lists" get shortened.

For example, a man or woman would like a new house—they say they've out grown their old one or perhaps they want a house with a bedroom on the main level. They could use a new or newer car. They would sure like to take the whole family to Disney to see Mickey and friends this coming spring. Or, maybe the husband would like a new set of Ping golf clubs and the wife would really love to buy a Michael Kor's pocketbook. They have a family meeting and decide on a plan of action. That afternoon the wife goes for her annual mammogram. Three days later she is in her doctor's office and discovers that she has a malignancy.

> *Adversity shortens our "want list."*

What do you suppose they want now? What matters now? They couldn't care less about a set of clubs, a car, a new house or a trip to Disney. All they want is for her to be well. Adversity always shortens our "want list." None of us ever want or welcome adversity but it sure helps us keep our priorities in line. Few experience the kind of adversity Paul dealt with day in and day out, since the day he became a Christian. I have a feeling that his ongoing dealings with difficulty helped him to learn contentment.

Contented people have great confidence in Christ. Paul writes in verse 13:

> *I am able to do all things through Him who strengthens me.*
> *(Phil 4:13)*

My mom had incredible confidence in Christ. That, in part, was why she was the most contented person I've ever known. She believed God knew everything about her. She was certain He had her name, address, and zip code down perfectly so that if she was intended to have something, He would see she got it. If she didn't get it, there was no disappointment because she didn't believe it was His will for her to have it. She lived and died believing He had her best interest at heart. When you believe that, you don't go around thinking somehow you have been short changed. Moma demonstrated all eight of the qualities or conditions I have mentioned in this chapter. And don't think for a moment that it's genetic, because I have seldom been very contented in my life.

My dad retired from the Army as a First Sergeant, so needless to say, we weren't wealthy people. We never lacked for anything, but there wasn't a lot to spare. My mother never complained. She may have expressed desires to my dad for things, but if she did, she did so in private. I never knew my mother to ask for a house, a car, clothes, vacations—anything. Even after all the kids were gone from home and money was far more available than it had once been, my Moma remained content. She was perfectly content to stay at home, play with her grandkids, and take care of her family. Her relationship with Christ and her family were all she needed to feel perfectly content. It doesn't get any better than that.

That's what I want for you, and especially, for me. Choose door number two!

QUESTIONS TO TALK ABOUT

1. If you had $10,000,000 what would you do with it?

2. How long do you think it would be before you found yourself discontent again?

3. Are you discontent? If so, why?

4. Who is the most contented person you know? Do they have a lot of worldly possessions? Ever asked them why they are so content or what the secret of their contentment is?

5. Do you know anybody with lots of stuff who is anything but content?

CHAPTER FIFTEEN

CHOOSING HOW I SPEND MY LIFE

For you are like smoke that appears for a little while, then vanishes. James 4:14b

A WHILE BACK MY GRANDDAUGHTER, Scout, and I went to the movies. We saw the animated movie, *Epic*. I won't try to describe a particular scene to you because I could never do it justice, but suffice it to say (or even better, rent the movie), if James had seen it, he would have said, "That's right; man is kinda like a fruit fly."

Time passes quickly for us. When I was a kid, it took a hundred years for Christmas to roll around; today it comes every six months. If you are thirteen, life may seem annoyingly long, but if you are eighty, you wonder where the time went. My dad turned to me a day or two after my mother passed and said, "It went so quickly. It doesn't seem possible that she's gone and our lives have passed." They were married sixty-four years.

Granted, some live longer than others. But don't kid yourself into believing that it lasts for any of us. The Psalmists said:

All my days were written in Your book and planned before a single one of them began. (Ps. 139:16)

So I don't have forever on this earth. Common sense, which is becoming less and less common, dictates I spend my time wisely. I especially like the way the Cotton Patch version of the New Testament captures Paul's thought in Ephesians 5:16 when it says,

Use your time as though you had to buy it.

You see, lots of us are as careless as a drunken sailor in spending our time, but most of us give a little more thought to how we spend our money. Most people want to believe they are getting their money's worth in making purchases. We shop for cars over a period of weeks or months, more often than not because we know this isn't a purchase we can afford to mess up. We read car magazines and talk to people who own the model car we are considering purchasing. Do we ever get careless with money? Of course. Typically, though, that happens when we believe we have a surplus. We receive a bonus. Somebody leaves us a large inheritance. We get a check back from the IRS.

Imagine I give you a million dollars, all in ones. Can you imagine what a huge pile that would be? If you had that many "ones" and you weren't careful, it would be so easy to become frivolous with your money. In view of all the cash laying around, it would seem as though you could waste some if you wanted to do so. As a prank, I can readily imagine some smokers and even a few of my non-smoker buddies rolling up a few ones and lighting up. Some of us would perhaps consider going to an upper floor of a building and letting it rain dollars on passersby below, just to see their reaction. Lots of us might pay way too much for some item we wanted because, after all, we have plenty. There's more where that came from.

Sadly, tragically even, that's how many people spend their time—as though they had a limitless supply. When you live day after day for years, why wouldn't you expect "there's more where that came from?"

With that in mind, may I make six recommendations?

LIVE PURPOSEFULLY, INTENTIONALLY, DELIBERATELY.

Don't just live aimlessly. Don't wander. Granted, in times of crisis you may have to put yourself in survival mode. Your goal may be just to survive the heartache. To cope with what you are enduring may be as good as you can expect in these difficult moments. But don't get stuck there. Don't let that become a way of life. Map out your steps; don't just get on a treadmill.

LIVE TO BRING GOD GLORY.

Isaiah says that is why all of us were made. How do I do that? It starts by acknowledging Him. Saying or acknowledging something like, "God You exist. I want to know You. I want to please You, to follow You. I will obey You. You are God and I am not. I will comply with Your wishes. I will follow You."

We live in a Christian culture that is willing to claim any form of acknowledgement of God as a valid profession of one's faith. I can do as little as check a box on a church membership card, repeat a prayer I don't understand, or jump in someone's pool at a youth rally, and we will find a way to convince ourselves that the miracle of conversion has transpired. But Jesus was never tempted to dumb down what He required of those who would be His disciples. He required denial, death, and a willingness to follow Him. Like Joshua, make a choice to follow Christ and thereby bring Him glory.

LIVE, LOOKING AND LISTENING FOR GOD.

God has spoken in a number of ways. He speaks generally when He shows up in creation. Whenever you see Him through creation, acknowledge Him. Look for Him as you walk along the shore. Spot Him in the heavens on a starry night. See evidence of His work when you hold that newborn.

Listen when He speaks specifically to you through His word. Allow Him to guide you, correct you, admonish you, rebuke you, and encourage you. That can only happen as you meet Him in His Word. Read His Word daily. And when you read, learn to listen for His voice. What is He saying to you? It's great to know what He has said to others, but better still to know what He is saying to you. Obey Him.

And don't be afraid to listen as He speaks to you personally. Some Christians have become so fearful of someone misinterpreting their personal experiences with God that they have almost discounted altogether God's ability to speak to us apart from His Word. While both scripture and experience indicate that He speaks to us on a personal basis on rare occasions, He does speak. That's one of the reasons we pray, isn't it? I am fearful that we have so discounted His ability to speak or our ability to understand what He says, that we seldom give much credence to the voice of God in our lives.

1 Samuel relates to us the story of God speaking one evening to Samuel while he is under the tutelage of Eli. Samuel reports to Eli, and asks what he might do for him and Eli tells him he hasn't called for him. It isn't until the third time that Samuel goes to Eli that the experienced priest realizes that God is speaking to young Samuel. The Bible even helps us understand why Eli has not immediately reached this conclusion. In 1 Samuel 3:1 the Bible says,

> *In those days the word of the Lord was rare and prophetic visions were not widespread.*

He speaks to us personally on rare occasion. But He does speak. Listen for His voice. Obey His voice.

A few weeks ago I called all of our church staff together and asked them, "Has there ever been a time in your life that God unmistakably spoke to you a message that was specifically for you?" Every person in the room recalled such a time. I talked with a few laymen in the days that followed and every person with whom I spoke said the same. No one heard an audible voice. Every person said, however, they were absolutely convinced that the word they felt in their heart was a word from God.

To be sure, know that God will never contradict Himself. His heartfelt word heard in prayer will always at least parallel what the Bible tells us. But there are times when He desires that you act in a particular fashion, to a particular circumstance. Don't be afraid to listen for His voice. I am convinced those will be some of the most rewarding moments of your life.

LIVE DOING WHAT GOD CREATED
AND PREPARED YOU TO DO.

You are unique. No one on this planet is exactly like you. You have unique DNA, you are unique physically, emotionally, intellectually, and spiritually. Your experiences to date, while similar to others in some respect, are different from anyone else's. God has used His design and your circumstances, experiences, and choices, to fashion you into the person you are.

Ask yourself, what has He created and prepared me to be and do? Am I doing that? If not, why not? It doesn't have to be grandiose in the eyes of the world. It just has to be meaningful. And, as you age, it may change. It may be tied to your vocation, but it may not be. It may be to help or encourage others. It may be to teach or counsel others. It may be to lead others or to be the right hand man of those who do. It may be to be an extraordinary follower. Whatever He has enabled you to do, do it. Find joy in it. Be happy about it. Don't be covetous or jealous of other's purposes. Be who you were meant to be and you will love life and find joy in it.

LIVE FOR SOMETHING BIGGER THAN YOURSELF.

In the movie, *Act of Valor,* a group of Navy SEALS are engaged in a mission when a terrorist lobs a hand grenade into the midst of their small outfit. One of the SEALS sees it and instinctively yells "grenade" while simultaneously throwing his body over the grenade. He manages to shield his fellow SEALS from the blast, but at great personal cost to himself. While this was just a movie, we all have read of those exact kind of acts of bravery among our military. People who make that sacrifice, do so instinctively. They do it without regret. The only way that response is possible, in my opinion, is that those people are living for something bigger than themselves. They value their lives less than they value their cause. Those brave men and women have made a commitment to their comrades from which they have no intention of ever walking away.

Have you become a part of something that means more to you than your own life? If not, I sure urge you to find something that will enable you to do that. Jesus said that is how a man finds life!

> Then Jesus said to His disciples, "If anyone wants to come with Me, he must deny himself, take up his cross, and follow me! For whoever wants to save his life will lose it, but whoever loses his life because of Me will find it. (Matt. 16:24-25)

The key to living a life that has meaning is to stop living for yourself. Live to please the Lord; live for others and you will find joy.

LIVE PREPARED TO DIE.

Lastly, live prepared to die. It always amuses me whenever I hear someone say, "If I die." Hey, you are going to die! Unless Christ returns before your death, you are going to die. Check the county records. For every person born, one dies! Great people, rich people, poor people, happy people, Christians, Muslims, Democrats, Republicans—we all die. Any thinking person ought to ask themselves, so what then? What will happen at death? Basically I believe two things occur. The first sounds a little redundant, but it's true—you stop living—physically. And, you aren't coming back! You aren't going to get a "do-over."

Because of what I do for a living, I meet lots of people who worry about leaving loose ends for their children to deal with, after their death. By that, I mean they want to have their affairs in order. They have a will, some make their funeral arrangements in advance, and they make sure, when possible, that their debts will be paid, and a little something is left over for their children. But here's the truth of the matter: when you die, whether you've picked out your casket or not, it's tough for your children. There's no easy way to say goodbye. If they loved you, they are going to hurt. If you can provide the money to cover those expenses, that is a blessing.

But if you are really concerned about leaving your affairs in order, make sure your relationships are what they should be. Don't leave your loved ones guessing about your feelings for them. Don't slip up and die on the outs with them because you were too stubborn to call and make things right. Mend relationships as you go. Do it while you are still breathing, because regardless what the spiritualists may try to tell you, you won't be sending messages back from the great beyond.

> *... make sure your relationships are what they should be.*

The second thing that happens at death is you settle the question you've considered all your life. Does God exist? Well, the debate is over. You get to meet Him—face to face.

Are you ready for that? If not, that's a question to which I would give serious consideration. The Bible confirms what we all know, that all men are sinners. But it also declares that Jesus bore our sins on the cross and that through Him we can have eternal life.

I have made innumerable bad choices in my life. If I were to be judged on the basis of my righteousness, I would surely be condemned. But I won't be judged. Not because I have managed somehow to make up for my bad choices; I couldn't in ten lifetimes. No, my confidence is not in myself but in Christ's willingness to pay my debt for me. He died for me on the cross, and I have made a conscious choice to ask for His forgiveness. I have repented of my sin and began years ago following Him. There are things I still hope to accomplish, see and do, but I assure you, I am ready to die. Are you?

QUESTIONS TO TALK ABOUT

1.   Do you have a bucket list? If so, what are some of the things you want to do before you die?

2.   What do you believe, at this point in time, is God's plan for your life?

3.   Have you had an experience where you believe God directed you specifically to do a particular thing?

4.   Are there any relationships that you need to do some work on before you die?

CHAPTER SIXTEEN

CHOOSING THE LONG HAUL OVER THE MOMENT

LET'S REVIEW FOR JUST A moment. Life is all about choices. The outcome of your life will be determined more by the choices you make than the circumstances under which you live. You have virtually no control over many of the circumstances of your life, but you, and only you, have everything to say about the choices you make in life.

The most important choice you will ever make is the choice of determining, "Do I live for the moment or do I live for the long haul?"

May I make a few observations regarding this choice that I believe you would do well to consider before making the choice?

The temptation will always be to live for the moment because it offers immediate gratification. I see the "now," but the future is hard to envision. Living in the moment typically makes me happiest in the next few moments. It requires the least restraint and offers the most immediate pleasure. But what is good in the short run may not prove best in the long run. Here, I am not just talking about the eternal but that which is later rather than sooner. (Do I party this evening with my friends or do I study?)

On the other hand, *What if there is no long haul?* What if I die prematurely? Someone gave me a placard a few years ago that said, "Life is uncertain; eat dessert first." What if there is no such thing as eternity?

But on the other hand, *What if eternity does exist?* Then life on this earth, even long life, is absolutely nothing by comparison. The scripture correctly says, "Life is like a vapor that appears for a little while and then vanishes away." Ask anybody over seventy, and they will tell you, life is short.

> *Living for the long haul, doesn't negate the opportunity to live at times in the moment.*

Living for the long haul, doesn't negate the opportunity to live at times in the moment. I always want to make sure I don't do something in the moment that I will live to regret, but there are times when I can live in the moment and live for the future simultaneously. I just can't do that all the time.

With those considerations in place, let me tell you why I believe it is wise to always make choices that serve you well over the long haul rather than simply in the moment.

Some squandered opportunities never return. There are lots of people who mistakenly believe, "If I mess it up, I'll just do it again." In golf, some amateurs play with what is known as a "mulligan." It's a free shot. Mess up? Do it over. It makes the game more interesting for some of us who aren't as good as others. The problem is, in real golf, there are no "do overs." Likewise, in life, there are many times when there are no do overs.

If you are a wood worker, you know that you can ruin a beautiful and quite expensive piece of mahogany simply by drilling a tiny hole in the wrong place. You can do your best to mask your mistake with wood putty and stain, but it won't ever be quite the same in most instances.

> Don't be deceived: God is not mocked. For whatsoever a man
> sows he will also reap, because the one who sows to his flesh

will reap corruption from the flesh, but the one who sows
to the Spirit will reap eternal life from the Spirit. (Gal. 6:7-8)

There are times when we can fully recover from our bad decisions,
but there are also times when the bad choice we make in school, marriage, on the job, or in a relationship—is never able to be salvaged. It's
an opportunity that is gone forever.

One is wise to always remember *the joy, happiness, and pleasure
of ill-conceived decisions is short-lived and forgotten, long after the pain of
those decisions is still felt.*

The famous parable of the prodigal son in Luke 15 is a beautiful
reminder of this truth. The prodigal squandered his inheritance in
what Jesus dubbed "riotous living." When money was gone, so were
the good times and his phony friends.

The son ends up in a pig pen, eating and sleeping with swine. Even
after going home and reconciling with his father, the relationship
between his brother and him remains broken and strained.

Unfortunately I can point you to hundreds of men and women
who have had affairs and lost everything that meant anything to
them—their children, spouse, job, and even many of their friends.

I could, likewise, introduce you to some very smart kids who are
in dead-end careers because they didn't take school seriously when
they had the chance, and now opportunities have passed them by.

In Luke 12:13-21, Jesus got pulled into a dispute between brothers
over an inheritance. Notice what He had to say:

> Someone from the crowd said to Him, "Teacher, tell my brother
> to divide the inheritance with me." "Friend," He said to him,
> "who appointed Me a judge or arbitrator over you?" He then told
> them, "Watch out and be on guard against all greed because
> one's life is not in the abundance of his possessions."

Then He told them a parable: "A rich man's land was very productive. He thought to himself, 'What should I do, since I don't have anywhere to store my crops? I will do this,' he said, 'I'll tear down my barns and build bigger ones and store all my grain and my goods there. Then I'll say to myself, "You have many goods stored up for many years. Take it easy; eat, drink, and enjoy yourself."

"But God said to him, 'You fool!' This very night your life is demanded of you. And the things you have prepared—whose will they be?'"

That's how it is with the one who stores up treasure for himself and is not rich toward God.

Two brothers were in a dispute over their inheritance. It doesn't take long for money to separate even brothers, does it? Jesus lets this man know immediately, this isn't a fight in which He wants to be caught in the middle. The best advice He can give them both is to avoid allowing greed to separate them. Life is not about how much or what you have. It is about relationships. Guard those and forget the money.

To help them see why this whole argument in which they find themselves is foolish, Jesus tells them a parable. He tells of a guy who is quite successful. The man in the parable has a banner year with his crops and wonders what he will do with the surplus of harvest. Think about it for a moment. What can he do? He can let them rot in the field—that doesn't seem very prudent. He could give them away. That would be generous but most business people would kind of cringe at the thought of giving that much profit away for naught. Or, he could build some more silos. That's what he does and if the truth be known, that's what most of us would do.

It wasn't the man's actions, but his thinking with which Jesus finds fault. He reasons because he has enough stored for the future that he will be here to enjoy it. Wrong! He dies and leaves it to another. The point is that a life consumed with stuff is a life that is ill conceived. Seek God first and foremost; make that your highest priority in life!

Take a look at one last scripture. In Matthew 16:24 Jesus says to His disciples,

> If anyone wants to come with Me, he must deny himself, take up his cross, and follow me. For whoever wants to save his life will lose it, but whoever loses his life because of Me will find it. What will it benefit a man if he gains the whole world yet loses his life? Or what will a man give in exchange for his life?

The best choice I ever made was the morning I decided to stop living for myself. That morning I gave my life away, and I gave it to the Lord Jesus Christ. I don't remember exactly what I said to God that morning as I fell on my knees and wept but it was something like this, "God, I have sinned against You and need for You to forgive me. I know that I have made a mess of things by trying to live the way I want to live, but from this day forward I am committing my life to You. I want to live for You. Thank you for paying for my sins by dying for me on the cross. I know this isn't going to be easy, but help me to live for You. In Jesus' name, Amen."

This book has been about choices. I wrote it because I've seen people make smart choices and live some incredible lives. And, unfortunately, I have also seen people make some bad decisions that cost them dearly. But here's the group that troubles me the most—those who hardly ever own any decision they've made. They have gone through life whining about all the bad things that have happened to them and never realized that most of their ill fortune was brought on by their own bad choices. More than trying to guide you in your decisions (and I admit I've tried to do that to some degree), it has been my hope that you would take ownership of your life and choices.

Choose wisely. Choose life!

It is my sincerest desire that this book has empowered you to recognize that you don't have to be a victim. If your family has created a cycle of failure, you can break it. If you have lived life in a destructive fashion, with God's help, you can change that. You don't have to continue down any path you are now on, unless you choose to do so. You can choose the life you want. The choices regarding your life are yours to make. Exercise care and caution. Choose wisely. Choose life!

QUESTIONS TO TALK ABOUT

1. Do you believe that there is life beyond the grave?

2. Why do you believe that people tend to live in the moment rather than live for the long haul?

3. If you were given a "do over" in life, how would you use yours?

4. If you could influence you children in regard to choices they will make in life, what would be your best advice to them?

5. Are there any decisions, as you look back over your life, that you blamed on someone else rather than take ownership or responsibility for?

CHAPTER SEVENTEEN

DECISION MAKING 101

MY DESIRE IN WRITING THIS book has been to help the reader understand the importance of making wise choices. Our choices impact our lives more than any other single factor in life. We have talked about a number of major decisions that most people face at one time or another. What about those choices, however, which are unique to our situation? What then?

Again, this won't be an exhaustive list of things to consider in making choices, but I do believe it will serve helpful in making the vast majority of decisions.

Partner with God. First and foremost, in my opinion, is what does God think? I discover His will on most issues by simply reading and applying His Word. I never want to choose to do anything that the scripture tells me is contrary to His will. For instance, His Word gives clear advice on whom not to partner with in business or marriage. It gives me endless instruction on how to handle disputes, engage in business, treat my body, handle my money, raise my children, earn the respect of my community, stay out of trouble legally, and, believe it or not, have a great sex life. People mistakenly believe the Bible, if followed, will lead to an austere life of denial. Nothing could be further from the truth. The Bible teaches you how to avoid pain and experience life the way God intended it to be enjoyed. Living God's way keeps you from much of the sorrow, guilt, loneliness, and failure that plague so many in our society today. I can honestly tell you that the people I know in life who live according to the scripture (they don't just claim to be Christians) are the most joyful, happy people I have ever met.

You may be thinking, but the Bible is such a large book, where do I begin? I am going to be straight up with you. The Bible is equally inspired from one book to another, but it isn't equally inspiring. If I want to know how to live and make wise decisions, every book will be helpful, but none more so than Proverbs. Proverbs is full of wisdom for living. Digest them verse by verse. Every verse is like a little puzzle. Figure out exactly what God is saying to you in each one. There are thirty-one chapters in the book. A man who wants to live skillfully should consider reading one every day for the rest of his life. In twelve months you would have read the book through twelve times.

The Sermon on the Mount in Matthew 5, 6, and 7 is likewise, a great source of inspiration and information regarding how Jesus wants us to live. In Colossians 3, the Apostle Paul gives us instruction on behaviors and attitudes that we are to rid ourselves of, as well as "put on." The narratives of the Bible, found in the Old and New Testaments, provide great examples on behavior that did and didn't work. That's what I love about the scripture; it doesn't sugar coat its characters, even its heroes. Someone has said, "Only a fool fails to learn from his mistakes." I would have to add, "Only a bigger fool fails to learn from the mistakes of others." I need not go down a path another has traveled, to know my destination will likely be the same.

Stay legal by a considerable margin. You think your driver's license picture looks bad? Wait till you see your mug shot. No one wants to start a prison ministry where you can't go home in the evenings. Stay legal and do so by a considerable margin. I see folks from time to time who want to live as close to the edge as they can. Dumb! In fact, if you ever hear someone try to sell you on an idea and they say at any point in their presentation, "And it's perfectly legal." Run! It's probably not perfectly legal and chances are it is illegal. Don't take chances with anything that could lead to your arrest, the embarrassment of your family or the loss of your reputation. Don't flirt with dishonest gain.

Always consider the consequences. Who could get hurt? What could go wrong? Can my life or the life of someone else be permanently altered? What if someone sends this letter, email or picture to someone else? If I got killed doing something stupid, how would that impact the lives of those who love me? If discovered in this activity, could it cost me my children, spouse, reputation, job? If I lose my scholarship, how would that impact my parents financially? If I say what I'm thinking, will this make matters better or worse? If I act on the anger I now feel, will it change anything in a positive way or am I likely to regret this later? Always consider the consequences!

Consider others. The line in Rick Warren's *Purpose Driven Church* I liked best and have quoted most often, came at the beginning of the first chapter: "It's not about you." Boy, what a great line! In every decision where it is remotely applicable, consider others. How will this decision impact my wife, husband, children, parents, co-workers, neighbors, friends, and even those who already think I'm a jerk?

Please hear what I'm saying. I want to always do the right thing; that may make some people around me unhappy, even those who love me. If it does, and I know it is the right thing, so be it. But there are times when I may be tempted to act in a fashion that is good for me and no one else, and I don't care how it impacts others. That's a wrong move. Live considerately of others, even if it keeps you from always doing what you would like selfishly to do. (Don't let your dog run loose or poop on someone else's yard, don't make your neighbor ask you to turn your music down, or don't make your family wait on your arrival in order to start Christmas dinner.)

Follow the leader. Bet I fooled you on this one. Don't blindly do whatever someone else asks you to do, but think about what that person you admire the most would do—the Leader—that guy or gal who you really think has his or her act together. What would they do? Having someone who is something of a hero to you can be very helpful. You can turn to them for advice, but if you know them pretty well, in most cases you can also discern what they would do in a given situation, and follow their example. I've employed this strategy any number of times in my life, right up to the present. My desire to be like those I admire and not disappoint them by acting foolishly has steered me to make some wise decisions that might not have gone so well otherwise.

Seek wise, forthright counsel. You want to employ this strategy sparingly but you do need to recognize when a decision demands the wise, forthright counsel of others. I have a staff member who loves to tell young guys who are a little cocky, "You don't know everything!" And he's right. The billionaire investor, Warren Buffett, has said he never invests in stocks he doesn't understand. There are lots of things I don't understand and when I don't, I don't have any problem turning to others for help.

I have purposefully used the adjectives "wise" and "forthright" twice now. In seeking counsel, I need to be honest with myself before I approach someone for advice. Ask yourself a couple of important questions: "Do I really want an honest opinion or am I looking for a rubber stamp?" "Do I trust what this person will tell me?"

If I do trust this person, and I am seeking an honest answer, why wouldn't I do what this person says? Some people may disagree with this strategy, but years ago I came to the conclusion that I wouldn't ask for advice unless I had confidence that the person I was going to ask for counsel would advise me correctly. So when I seek counsel, I almost always take the advice of the one giving it.

I don't want to ask someone for advice who is afraid of either offending me or throwing a wrench into my plans. I am asking for advice because I have doubts regarding my opinion. I don't want a "yes" man to tell me what I'd like to hear in the moment. I want someone who loves me enough to be honest with me and protect me from making a bad decision.

Don't sweat the small stuff. Marriage is a big decision—whether or not to get onions on my burger, isn't! My goal is to marry once, but I will be back at the Beacon Drive-In again. Learn to make decisions by spending an appropriate amount of time considering your options. Don't keep the waiter at your table for his or her entire shift; let them go make a buck. But by the same token, don't buy a house if you haven't compared it to at least a few others.

Pull the trigger. Every decision requires thought. As I have said, some more than others. But in all matters, those of importance and those of less importance, there comes a time to pull the trigger. The only way anyone can ever conclude before they make a decision that it is the perfect one is to know they have perfect information. And the only ones capable of having perfect information are God and, well, I guess that's all. And in case you haven't notice, you aren't God. So you won't have the luxury of perfect information. Even so, make a decision. If you can't do that with a measure of comfort, then pass. There's no shame in saying I don't feel comfortable making this decision. Pass it on to someone else, abandon the process, but don't suffer unendingly from paralysis by analysis, which only serves to frustrate you and those around you.

Consider your options. We are never limited to the first option we consider. On matters of consequence, I like to use "think tanks" to consider my options. Where I might see two or three options on my own, a group of creative thinkers will invariably produce a number of viable options. In addition to the options we name I can always choose to delay a decision, make no decision, or pass on an idea altogether. Some ideas that look promising initially don't appear to be so smart when I flesh them out a little. I don't like tabling something indefinitely either, but there is wisdom in tabling a decision at times for a specified season. It could be the idea is good but the timing is bad. The important thing to always keep in mind is that I have a choice. I don't have to do something because someone else thinks I should. Don't be pressured into a decision you will regret.

I've always felt a little bad for the girl who gets asked on national television in front of a stadium full of people if she would marry some fellow. I'm sure the vast majority of the time, the answer is a foregone conclusion, and she may not be that surprised (other than by the setting in which the question is popped). But what if she had been having second thoughts? Or worse still, what if this is some guy's way of pressuring some girl to do something she either hasn't seriously considered or doesn't really want to do? That's when, if we could freeze time for just a moment, I'd like to whisper in her ear, "You have a choice. This guy's request doesn't necessitate an immediate response on your part. You don't have to say, 'I will.'"

> *Make a good choice! In fact, make lots of them.*

But more often than not, the forfeiture of one's right to choose doesn't come in front of 80,000 onlookers in a stadium. No, it's more likely to come at an off campus party, around a water cooler at work, a client's office where you want to make that sale, in a lounge on an out of town business trip, or in committee meeting at church. But if you forfeit your right to choose for yourself, understand clearly, it's on you. You had a choice, you just didn't exercise it. So don't blame others. Take responsibility for your life. Make a good choice! In fact, make lots of them.

QUESTIONS TO TALK ABOUT

1. What do you believe are the three most important factors to consider in making a decision?

2. Who do you typically turn to for counsel when you have a difficult decision to make?

3. Have you ever forfeited your right to make the choice you wanted to make because you felt pressured to do so?

4. Can you identify some places where that has happened?

5. Why do you think it is so hard at times to say no to a request that you don't want to do?

For more information about
Dr. Ralph Carter
&

You Make The Call
Choices That Make or Break Us
please visit:

www.brushycreek.org

www.facebook.com/DrRalphCarter

@ralphcarter2

....

For more information about
AMBASSADOR INTERNATIONAL
please visit:

www.ambassador-international.com
@AmbassadorIntl
www.facebook.com/AmbassadorIntl